MW01483837

For the Love of HER Life

Autumn Edition

Compiled by Elizabeth Dyer

Preface by Kit Hinkle

Contributions from the Writing Team at aNew Season Ministries

Jill Byard, Teri Cox, Elizabeth Dyer, Karen Emberlin, Erika Graham, Kit Hinkle, Nancy Howell, Linda Lint, Katie Oldham, Sheryl Pepple, Sherry Rickard, Sarah Rodriguez, Leah Stirewalt, Liz Anne Wright, Rene Zonner

www.anewseason.net

Cover photo by Heavenly Eye

DEDICATION

You know the walk of solitude after losing your husband. You long for comfort from those who know your ache and can offer the kind of Hope and encouragement that can only come from the Lord through voices of those who have been there.

May you be blessed with our voices as you climb out from this difficult season. May you bless another when she walks in aNew Season, needing comfort during the early stages of loss.

Job 29:13b

Making the widow's heart sing for joy

Preface:

We've talked about placing a devotional book in the hands of widows since the start of A Widow's Might in 2009 and well into the birth of our umbrella ministry, aNew Season. Finally—here it is. When I think of all the ladies not yet online now being able to access these writings, my heart melts.

I picture **For the Love of HER Life**, our book of daily devotions, as a night-table book. One that perhaps someone got for her as a gift of love, knowing how much she is hurting. And at first it sits next to her, unopened.

Until at some point, she's up late at night and needs to hear from other widows. Finally she'll pull it from her night table to begin reading, letting the comfort of Christ wash over her1..

These daily devotionals come straight from our website. They have been proven over the years to bring comfort—the kind that lasts beyond the feel-good hug or reassuring smile, because they bring the comfort of God's Truth.

aNew Season Ministries ministers in the trenches of grief and beyond grief into victorious living through a walk with Christ. For the widow, when it seems no one else understands because they haven't lived it, aNewSeason.net is just a click away and able to minister to her.

We pray that this devotional becomes a way for a widow's friends and family to reach out to her. How many times have I been asked to mentor a widow, speak to her—tell her life isn't over. How many times have a widow's loved ones begged me to let her know that she has purpose and there are healthy ways to deal with grief?

And I do. And so do all the writers on our team.

But what about the widow who hasn't physically come across our path?

This devotional book can be given to her right there when the loss is fresh. It's like giving her a whole network of many women who have successfully navigated grief--women of many ages and situations with one thing in common—the knowledge that Christ is the answer to healing.

When the funeral is finished and everyone has gone home, she will eventually find herself in that place—face to face with her solitude. That's when her friends and family will want this devotional, written by many, to comfort her. As she reads through story after story, she'll get it. She's not alone. Many have walked before her—joyfully.

We've decided to publish these devotionals in three month seasonal cycles. We have enough for a year-long daily devotional, but to publish it in one book would make for a large book unless we abridged the writer' work or made the font so small it would become hard to read.

We pray you or your loved one will be blessed by these writings and hope to engage with you at our conferences or online at anewseason.net

God bless you!

~Kit Hinkle~

Prologue:

My prayer is that, as you read these daily devotions, you will be encouraged to live life again. You are a beautiful daughter of the King. He has more left for you to experience and give to others in this life. The writers at A Widow's Might/aNew Season are so blessed with the opportunity to share our writings with you as we journey together on the path of widowhood. Your heart will sing again.

~Elizabeth Dyer~

Introduction:
Autumn

To the reader of our devotionals for the months of September, October, and November:

Autumn brings a warm glow of orange, red and yellow leaves as a brisk wind swirls about branches that reach for a brilliant blue October sky. That wind can caress you with memories of pumpkin carvings and walks with your dear one along paths paved with a carpet of color. But it can also leave you feeling stripped—like the branches on that wind-swept tree. Remember the tree is not bare forever. It will be warmed, like you by aNew season of Son. We pray that while you wait for this new warmth, you cloak yourself with our devotions on God's Word spoken through us, a dozen widows who have been through what you are going through. Let us bring you into our conversation—show you how our fellowship with each other and the Lord made us whole once again.

~Kit Hinkle and Elizabeth Dyer~

September

September 1
Joy Comes in the Morning
By Nancy Howell

I will praise you, Lord, because you rescued me.
You did not let my enemies laugh at me.
Lord, my God, I prayed to you,
And you healed me.
You lifted me out of the grave;
You spared me from going down to the place of the dead.
Sing praises to the Lord, you who belong to him;
Praise his holy name.
His anger lasts only a moment,
But his kindness lasts for a lifetime.
Crying may last for a night,
But joy comes in the morning.
Psalm 30:1-5 NCV

Shock. Disappointment. Grief. Pain. Unable to breathe. Sad. Angry. Needy. Bewildered. Paralyzed. Hurt. In denial. Bitter. Helpless. Frozen. Miserable. Unhappy. Sorrowful. Depressed. Devastated. Upset. Unsettled. Full of Angst. Heartbroken. Overwhelmed. Shattered. Distraught. Overcome. Upset. Distressed.

Dear sisters, above is but a sampling of the emotions I have experienced, up close and personal, since my unimagined journey as a widow began. I'm betting that each of you can identify with them. Most of you can likely add in a few of your own.

Grief doesn't follow a set schedule. Every

grieving person is different. There's no textbook outline for the path a widow should take, no set timetable. Those emotions I listed above? They aren't pretty. They aren't easy. And they sure don't make you the life of the party.

But they are necessary. Processing grief means working through the pain, the shock, the sadness, the depression, and whatever else is thrown your direction. Whether you choose to tackle it alone, with trusted friends and family by your side, with a counselor or pastor, through writing and blogging, or some combination thereof—you must acknowledge it.

By accepting the emotions, you can claim them. They are a part of who you now are, although with God's help, they don't have to define you.

In the midst of all of the bad, there is still good. God is there. He always was, and always will be. He's just waiting for you to ask for help. And the comfort He has for you holds the potential to heal you and your family.

I asked. I prayed. I clung to the Scriptures, spent time on my knees. And you know what? God didn't abandon me. He answered my prayers. He showed me that life can still be good.

Oh, healing didn't happen overnight, as I prayed it would. I had to walk the walk. After all this time, I'm still walking it. There are days I feel like I've been catapulted back to the raw emotions of my initial loss. There are moments I cry big old tears as I wonder what could have been.

However, there are also moments I feel optimistic. There are flashes of normalcy, of constructive, affirming feelings. Before losing my husband, I may have taken some of these for granted. But never again. Laughter. Happiness. Contentment. Bliss. Thankfulness. Hope. Enjoyment. Amusement. Gladness. Glee. Appreciation. Joy.

Just last week, I heard sounds almost foreign to me, some I haven't heard in quite some time. Propped up on pillows in my bed, I enjoyed the last of my coffee as I waited for my boys to finish showering. In a couple minutes, I would spring into action, becoming fashion consultant, drill sergeant, chef, negotiator, and chauffeur. While silently giving thanks for the beautiful morning, I heard it—singing. Both boys were singing in the shower. They are *happy*. Happy enough to belt out lyrics at seven in the morning. I cried tears of joy. The Scriptures, again, are right—joy *does* come in the morning.

Sisters, by embracing whatever emotions we have, we can work through our pain. And on the other side of that pain are a beauty and a peace that only God can provide.

Joy awaits you—I promise. He is a God of restoration. Your life won't be the same, but it will be beautiful, nonetheless. Joy comes in the morning.

Father God, thank You for this joy that awaits me. Thank You for restoration and beauty that only You can provide. I know my life will never be the same again but I also know that You make things beautiful. I am looking for this beauty and joy today. Amen

September 2
Work for Soul Rest
By Katie Oldham

Let us, therefore, make every EFFORT to enter that rest...
Hebrews 4:11 NIV

Sounds counterintuitive, doesn't it? Work more to rest. Give MORE effort to experience LESS stress. But that's exactly what Hebrews 4:11 says.

My single-mommy heart desires the restfulness God promises. But how can I make every effort when I'm already out of energy?

My answers come clearly from His Word: *Do not worry, worship Him, trust in the Lord with all my heart.* It sounds easy enough!

But I still strive and struggle to find real soul rest. I worry, stress and fret about where my girls will go to school, how I'll ever equip them with all they need when their Daddy died, and I'm already torn at the seams. Sometimes it's a wonder how my house stays standing in the midst of *my petty, stress-torn little storm!*

You know how this feels, right? We ALL seek solace for our lives. But, how can we get our worn-out, human hands on the deep rest we want in this world?

God says we must make an effort to realize this lasting respite we long for-the kind this world's incapable of offering.

I want it! So, I seek to obey.

Let us, therefore, make every effort to enter that rest so that no

one will fall by following their example of disobedience.
Hebrews 4:11 (NIV)

We learn from our ancient ancestors, those Moses led away from Egypt, to remain close to the Lord to receive our reward. A reward of rest. Soul rest. **Even our Father fully rested on the seventh day.** He generously extends His blessing to those of us who obey (reference Hebrews 4: 3-10).

I obey!

I **work** every day to live a little closer to the Lord. Inhale stress, exhale prayer. **Dive** into morning devotion. God-pleasing **words** as I multitask making meals and monitoring homework. I **work** my way through the Word to live close to Christ and find this rest promised to me. **Promised to YOU!**

It's strange what I find when I work a little harder. You'd think making more effort would wear me out more. But instead I'm refreshed. I feel at peace. I walk with deeper intention. I feel a sense of more time when I trust God's promise!

He creates space in my mind, my soul and even my schedule when I work to live well with Him in my heart!

Try it for yourself. *WORK to live close to Christ and He'll take care of the rest by providing real soul rest!*

Continually seeking God offers calm and confidence in the course of any kind of day. By pursuing Him I'm in closer touch with my purpose…and that, my Friends, feels peaceful because it's right where I belong.

That's it! Living close to the Lord provides a deep and personal peace, an authentic peaceful purpose. We cease hearing what the world wants of us. We stop striving towards social standards and exorbitant self-expectations. **We finally learn who God wants us to be simply by staying comfortably close to Him.**

Once we acquaint ourselves with God's plan for our lives, we're in sync with Him and we rest.

Our souls rest when we're living in line with Him.

We obey and He carries the worries away. Now and right on into eternity.

We make every effort and experience REAL SOUL REST in surrendering to Him.

So, yes, I'm still this single mom striving too hard, exhausted at the end of the day, wrought with worry. Seems I'm a slow learner after all. But I'm calling on Christ to carry me through. I'm leaning on the Lord to be the spiritual Father and Husband of my household. I'm making an authentic effort and in each inevitable failure, *I find myself at the foot of the Cross forgiven and receiving the reward of rest.*

It's my prayer for you, too. That you work each day to live close to Christ. That you surrender your life into the capable hands of your Creator.

It's there in the rewarding work and the sweet surrendering where you'll find peace, real soul rest.

September 3
A True Widow's Mite
By Kit Hinkle

He also saw a poor widow put in two very small copper coins.

"Truly I tell you," he said,
"this poor widow has put in more than all the others."
Luke 21:2-3 NIV

After going through the first few years of being without my husband, I walked a friend through her murky waters of divorce. It was tough on her on many fronts, but one of the worst moments for her was the legal arbitration over the division of assets. She asked for my help because she felt unable to contain her emotions enough to think logically. She was not only distraught about her marriage ending, but also fearful of facing a future without a husband to depend on financially.

When all was agreed upon, she thanked me. The final settlement was more than fair, and gave her some assurance that her finances were, for the time being, secure.

That's when I turned to her and suggested, "Before you go on with your life, get alone and pray about how much of this settlement the Lord wants you to give back to Him."

Fear overtook her. "I'm lucky to even have enough to lean on for a while. I don't have anything to give to the church."

She didn't understand what the giving was about. "This isn't about money. It's about what money will do to you."

That's when I shared with her the single most critical decision I made when becoming a widow—**I gave part of what I was given as a widow back to the Lord.**

No matter how secure or insecure your finances are as a widow or single mom, God is clear on what your attitude towards money should be. You cannot serve both God and money, and if you allow fear over your finances to overtake you, you're serving the wrong god.

That's why, when I started my new life as a widow, I did so by turning over a significant amount back to my church. It was a great step in opening my heart to further giving—a path that led me to having enough confidence to still eagerly turn over a normal tithe from my social security check to the church and continue to give even further to the needy.

I tell you this as I told my friend: I don't feel I can afford to give what I give. I really need to watch every dime because I've made a financially difficult choice to not work so I can homeschool my children. My nest egg has to last at least through the raising of these children, with hopefully enough to help with my retirement.

While giving every week is sacrificial, it has an amazing effect on my heart. It's as though each week, when I write out a check, I'm making a loud statement to the enemy. I'm saying, "Satan, get out of my life." And I'm saying to money, "You don't control me! Christ, through my actions, controls you."

And guess what? It works! Rarely do worries over finances have me up at night—even when something disrupts my finances. Giving helps me remember not to worry, but trust.

Now, before you go thinking that it is just because I'm "wired" that way, I want you to understand—I'm not. We all worry. It's part of our sinful nature to worry. It's a resulting action of our nature which Christ commands us not to do

(Matthew 6:25). The peace I have over giving wasn't there before.

When I lost Tom, I worried. So much so that when the life insurance company sent me claim forms after Tom's death, I filled them out with trembling hands and RAN to the post office to have them overnighted to the benefits department. I was terrified at the thought that anything could disrupt any possibility that I'd have to raise these boys without financial help.

I knew in my heart that my fear was unfounded. The boys and I are under the Lord's care—not the care of money. **Continual giving is my way of exercising that part of my heart that has learned to trust Him more and more**.

I know that some of us are comfortable and well-provided for while others are scraping to get along month by month. But we all have heart "muscles" that need to be exercised by trusting God more and more.

Father God, open the eyes of our hearts in the matters of money. Help us to understand the power in a widow's mite. No matter how big or how small our material fortune is, help each of us to remember it all belongs to You and that by continually giving part of it back to You each week we reclaim our trust in Your care, and only in Your care. In Jesus' Name, Amen.

September 4
Drilling Him Into Your Heart
By Rene Zonner

...you are precious to me. You are honored and I love you.
Isaiah 43:4 (NLT)

I realize these words are true. I know God loves me. Still, there are times in which I feel unlovable, unworthy…even alone. Why?

Friends, for many of us, the deaths of our spouses stir up feelings of no longer feeling special, set apart, or chosen by another. But through Scripture, we are able to see truth. God tells us time and again we are indeed treasures, precious to Him. We are loved and chosen.

However, knowing the truth and actually living it are two separate things. How do we transition from head knowledge (the knowing) of God's love to heart knowledge (the feeling) of that love?

There are many ways, I'm sure. The following works for me. I call it DRILL and it has become second nature to me in my journey to truly feel the depth of God's love. DRILL stands for:

Dive in, **R**ecord, **I**nvoke, **L**ook Around, and **L**ook Beyond:

Dive In!

First and foremost, dive into God's Word. Think of the Bible as God's personal love letter to you. Surrounding ourselves with the words of love He gives us is an important beginning step.

Record!

I keep a green leather journal with me at all times, small enough to fit in my purse. When I read a Scripture that touches me, as if God is speaking to me personally, I write it down.

The journal is not just for Scripture—if a song, or a quote from a book, devotion, or sermon touches my heart or gets my attention, it goes in, as well.

It's always close by. When God speaks to me through every day happenings, I immediately write it down.

Invoke!

If I ever doubt my place in God's heart, or feel loneliness begin to weigh me down, I simply pull out that journal. Each time I read a "note" from God, I take one more step beyond knowing His love in my head to truly feeling it in my heart.

Look Around!

By writing in my journal, I have gotten into the habit of looking around for examples of His love in my everyday life. When you begin truly looking, you will be astonished—it's everywhere! Talk about overwhelming evidence.

Look for God everywhere! He can be found in a phone call from a friend at just the right moment, a devotion speaking exactly to your feelings—He can even be seen in the timing of a check in your mail. Rest assured! God is thinking of you and loving you.

Look Beyond!

It's not just the good things happening to us. Looking at disappointments, or hurtful actions of others from the right perspective can show you how God protects you or takes care of you. Choose to see all as evidence of His perfect love, even when, in the midst of those moments, you may not be able to see the good. When you actively seek God, you will be overwhelmed by what you find!

Dear friends, we have a unique opportunity in

this season of widowhood. We can really focus on God in ways we couldn't when our loved one was still with us. None of us would have chosen this journey—nevertheless, allow God to make the most of it.

If, like me, you identified your self-worth and validation by your husband and your marriage, losing that safe sanctuary is difficult. It's also a chance to build your confidence through God's unwavering love for you. The process takes time and energy from you--but the reward will be worth it.

I believe someday God may bless me again with marriage. Before that happens, I must learn to seek validation and self-worth only from God. For me to be my own person, the person God wants me to be, I want to go into future relationships—friends, family, possibly marriage—enjoying the full pleasure of what they are meant to be.

Why don't you take this journey alongside me? Let's become secure in God, first and foremost, so that no matter what else the world throws our direction, we have assurance in both our heads and in our hearts. We. Are. Chosen.

Heavenly Father, I pray I will not just know with head knowledge about Your love for me, but also truly feel it deep in my heart and soul. Speak to me through Scripture, music, and the words of others, so I may hear Your personal message to me. Help me have an open heart and mind to the evidence of Your love all around me. Flood my soul, dear Father, with Truth, so it becomes not just something I know, but something I feel. Thank You in advance for the confident, secure and chosen woman I am becoming in You. Amen

September 5
Flying
By Erika Graham

For you formed my inward parts;
you knitted me together in my mother's womb.
I praise you, for I am fearfully and wonderfully made.
Wonderful are your works; my soul knows it very well.
My frame was not hidden from you,
when I was being made in secret,
intricately woven in the depths of the earth.
Your eyes saw my unformed substance;
in your book were written, every one of them,
the days that were formed for me,
when as yet there was none of them.
Psalm 139:13-16 ESV

My children and I take a family of "four" vacation to the same place every summer now. It has become a treasured NEW tradition; one of the many I'm creating as we move forward.

One of the highlights of our most recent vacation was going to our favorite beach. On the third day of this trip, there was a threat of rain and it was chilly. I decided to brave it anyway, and grabbed TWO kites and a soccer ball. As we pulled down the two lane road, I realized I might be the only person thinking it might NOT rain. My ten year old daughter and twin seven year old sons groaned a bit as we unloaded. So I prayed half-heartedly for no rain. We settled in and some bickering began. My no rain prayer petition became a bit more serious.

Once we figured everything out the wind began to pick up, so it was perfect for kite flying. There was a problem though, I purchased two kites and thought we could "buddy" up and share. I definitely had some twin brain (it's a fact, twins drain your brain twice as fast) issues that morning. They weren't in the mood to share. So, I explained they had to figure it out or the kites were going back to the car. Quickly, they had worked out a plan. My daughter and my dominant son convinced my very placid, happy-go-lucky son to let them have a go at the two kites while he "watched." He as usual complied with a smile.

After a few minutes they had the kites up and flying. I watched as the observing twin marveled at their skills for a little while. Then he lost interest. I felt terrible that he had no kite of his own and the guilt set in on my morning "twin" brain. But instead of complaining, he began to look around and fumble through our stuff. Before I knew it he had created his own kite. He was off running around, hooting and hollering, while his make-shift kite invention soared behind him.

I sat there in awe of my three uniquely and wonderfully made kids. I watched as my cautious girl soared her kite closer in and carefully monitored it often. My dare-devil boy was flying high and free above where he paid it little mind. Then there was my precious, inventive son who can make his own fun out of anything.

After my beloved husband's death, I find it important and even helpful for their grief process to tell them what traits or idiosyncrasies they have that were their daddy's. But inwardly I worry. My mommy heart is frightened by what they "could" inherit. He had so many wonderful qualities, but he also suffered greatly in his last few years. I also worry for them and the weight they will carry because their father committed suicide. It's my mom heart and I know my mom heart lets Satan in.

As I watched my three amazing children and how they each flew their kites differently, God reminded me of the verses above. He's formed them each, He's planned their days, and He knows their innermost beings better than I ever will. He is their all in all; He knows their beginning, and their end. I don't have to worry! They are each uniquely and wonderfully made and I can fully trust Him for all their days. No matter what traits they may inherit, they are in HIS hands!

I sat savoring my three blessings and their unique kite flying techniques and meditating on God's words, and such a sense of relief settled in. I'm not burdened by the traits my kids might inherit from either of us. But, I'm freed by a God who's so much bigger than our flesh. I can trust Him and His plan for them. I am so grateful for His promises, provision, and love for my kids and for me.

Father God, help me trust You and Your plan for me and for my loved ones. Open my eyes to Your promises and love today. Amen

September 6
You're With Me
By Linda Lint

I will never leave you, nor forsake you.
Hebrews 13:5 KJV

It felt strange to be sitting there, eating alone – in the same booth where my beloved and I had sat so many times, sharing a burger, a large order of fries, and conversations about our daily lives.

One evening stood out in my memory. Upon arriving here, we saw what could gently be described as "a homeless man" standing by the door. His eyes were empty, his shoes didn't match, his gloves had holes (and it was cold).

It was difficult to eat, knowing he was outside in the cold. The counter people said others had provided food and coffee. That knowledge eased our minds a bit until they mentioned how they had the food taken out to him to avoid having him come inside to eat.

The next morning my husband returned to the restaurant and insisted the man come inside to join him for a meal. The man resisted. "They don't want me in there," he said.

My husband opened the door and ushered the man inside, ignoring some strange looks, and whispered comments. *"It's ok,"* he said. *"you're with me"*.

That was my beloved. While others were willing to buy food for the man to eat outside in the cold, he brought him inside to the warmth.

We wanted to do more. Gathering gloves, a warm hat, a sweater, and a pair of shoes, we headed out to give the items to him, only to be disappointed. He was no longer there.

"He just moved on," someone said. "You know how it is with the homeless."

Over the next several days, through conversations with various business people and the local police, it appeared that he had really "disappeared". He was there - and then simply gone.

We put the experience behind us, but thought of it often. It was getting colder, and we couldn't forget those mismatched shoes and gloves with holes. My beloved drove around town looking for him; disappointed at not being able to give him the warmer clothing.

Then one morning, as I joined my husband for coffee at the kitchen table, I noticed he was quite distracted and a little shaken. With tears in his eyes, he described a dream he had about Heaven. He hadn't died, just got to look in on heaven.

In front of him was the throne. God was on the throne, with Jesus at His right hand. My husband could vaguely make out the figure at God's left hand. Walking closer he recognized who it was—the homeless man!

Now, ten years later, I have come to see another purpose for God sending this man into our lives. God wants to remind me that I am not really alone.

As a widow, I have many days of feeling as if I am outside in the cold and have that feeling of "they don't want me in there". I no longer have what I had for twenty-five years—that blessing of my husband's love and his unspoken words to me – "It's ok, you're with me". And it was ok, because we were together – when the storms came, when hail damaged the roof, when finances were tight and especially when we had a burger and fries.

Being alone these last two years has not been easy; yet, I have come to realize Jesus has been speaking those same words to me every day. *Jesus says "It's ok, you're with me. I am with you, right beside you – in those lonely times, in those places that are strange, in those places where tears come – and, yes, even when you have a burger and fries".*

Everyday Jesus makes the same promise to you as well, dear sister – *"I will never leave you, or forsake you".* Jesus says to you – *"It's ok, you're with ME"!*

Father God, thank You for all the years of love my beloved and I shared. I thank You for Your daily presence in my life. Please continue to walk with me and guide me as I go forward into the future You have planned for me. Amen

September 7
Bent, But Not Broken
By Nancy Howell

I have been a widow for a while but it is still hard. I have days that are filled with tears, sadness, and "what-ifs." I look at my two sons, growing up without their dad, and it breaks my heart.

During the first year, I had countless times I just wanted to give up. I would've liked nothing better than to have drawn the curtains, stayed in my pajamas, curled up in bed alongside my cat, with a box of tissues, and cried. Cried for what I've lost. Cried for what could have been. Cried for what my boys will grow up without. I could've done that for days.

But I didn't have that luxury. Two boys, only eight and nine when their dad died, now had only me. I was the "new sheriff in town", the one making all the decisions, the new head of our household. They were looking to me for strength and courage, for reassurance that we were going to be okay. Overwhelmed, I went on automatic pilot, doing what needed to be done. God helped me with every decision—whether big, little, easy, or exasperating. As I look back, those first months were a blur.

Up was down, down was up. But in the midst of the Texas-sized tornado that our life was after losing our husband and daddy, we surprisingly found ourselves still standing. Our roots were stronger than I ever imagined. And as we struggled to deal with a year of "firsts" without Mark, my children and I recognized our God wasn't going to let us break.

I'll be blunt: there were instances I felt certain we'd splinter into a million pieces. Facing birthdays, a wedding anniversary, Thanksgiving, Christmas—all in the first five months—was unbelievably difficult, but we endured. Through all of our pain, grief, and sadness, God is with us, steady and true. His love never fails. We see He's not going anywhere.

In my family's case, we're still bent from our loss. We've huddled together against the wind, the rain, and the elements that threatened to uproot us. I can see that we are beginning to unbend a bit, if ever so slightly. We appreciate that our blessings are numerous even now. The sun still shines upon us, and life continues. Each day we encounter grace in many forms.

We will never be the same as we were before. That's okay. We trust that God knows what He's doing, and that good will sprout from the bad. I'm forever thankful for the Rock upon which we're planted. I don't mind being a bit bent, as long as I'm still growing in God's eyes.

And I am convinced that nothing can ever separate us from God's love. Neither death nor life, neither angels nor demons, neither our fears for today nor our worries about tomorrow— not even the powers of hell can separate us from God's love.
Romans 8:28 NLT

Father, I pray that my circumstances will be used for Your glory, and that the comfort You've given my family is something I can share with others in similar situations. I'm so glad that You love me enough to keep me standing, and make me flexible enough to bend when necessary. Amen

September 8
Huffing and Puffing Ahead

By Elizabeth Dyer

Physical training is good,
but training for godliness is much better,
promising benefits in this life and in the life to come.
                                    I Timothy 4:8 NLT

Training.

I shudder at that word. It means I need help. That I don't know what I am doing.

My husband used to "train" for marathons. He "trained" for triathlons. People go for "training" when they are in the work-place. Dogs get "trained". Why does "training" put a bad taste in my mouth? Maybe because I like to think I can do it.

So when I started on an exercise program recently, I huffed and puffed on the treadmill. I finally made it to week five, day two of my exercise program. If exercise holds benefits here on earth, why am I so reluctant to strive for those benefits? My body groans and hesitates to move ahead to week five, day three!

I want to stop because I know it gets harder. Physical training is TOUGH! I will have to jog longer, sweat a lot more, and all this huffing and puffing is practically embarrassing!

Sometimes I feel like the "huffing and puffing" I do through grief is practically embarrassing too! But it's what I have to do to move ahead through the stages of grief--you know... denial, anger, bargaining, depression, and acceptance.

When I find myself struggling to progress through these stages, it's usually because I am afraid to move ahead. Afraid that moving ahead means moving further away from the life I had with my husband. Moving further away from the last time I held him in my arms. Moving further away from the last time we kissed. I don't want to let those memories fade away.

As I move along in my grief, those events DO begin to fade. I start to wonder what Mark's voice sounded like when he called me. If I leave the early stages of grief and move to the acceptance stage, will I forget the smell of his cologne? Will I remember the way his hand felt in mine?

So today I moved to week six in the exercise program. I won't be ready for a 5K anytime soon, but I am moving FORWARD in my progress through my journey. And along this journey, I will encounter memories. Good, sweet memories. Hard, painful memories. All of them need to be handed over to God. I need to ask Him what He wants me to do with them. How does He want to use my memories to bring glory to Him? I can't even begin to imagine that right now since it's only been six months since Mark's death.

But, Lord willing, I am getting further along each day. I never imagined I could make it six months. But then, really, what option did I have? I HAVE to make it. I have a house full of kids who need a parent, even one who cries at dinner. Even one who is flawed and sinful. I am all they have right now. Kind of like Moses in that regard. Moses was all God provided to lead the Israelites to the Promised Land, and he was flawed. He had issues.

When you struggle this week and are having trouble seeing any progress, remember I Timothy 4:8 and see your grief journey as perfecting you, and push through the stages of your grief as you would through an exercise of the body. Pray that God will help you see progress in your desert to where He can use you and your memories to bring glory to Himself. That will be the godliness He desires in us here in the present life and in the life to come. And I hope our desert part of the journey doesn't last for forty years!

Heavenly Father, I am really struggling with my grief today. I don't want to forget, but I don't want to move ahead either. I am afraid, God. Give me eyes to see Your love today. Give me true acceptance of my past and develop in me the godly character that I need for this life on earth and for the life to come with You in heaven. Thank You for the memories I have of my husband, the good ones and the bad ones. Use my memories to bring glory to You and bring others to know Your love. Amen

September 9
Leave the Grain and Rest!
By Kit Hinkle

And you shall not strip your vineyard bare,
neither shall you gather the fallen grapes of your vineyard.
You shall leave them for the poor and for the sojourner:
I am the LORD your God.
Leviticus 19:10 ESV

I was one of those kids who rarely had to do any serious cleaning. My parents had a Brady Bunch style "Alice" housekeeper-nanny-type who tidied up whatever spills us kids made.

You might be thinking "lucky kid" or "spoiled kid". But it's that second label that makes the first one so inaccurate. My husband understood that and liked that I wasn't a perfectionist. He was content that the house was tidy and sanitary and fashionably decorated. "Any more than that," he'd say, "and I wouldn't be able to relax."

Relax. Rest. Renewal.

Isn't that part of the Lord's plan? I was watching a pastor talk about this last week at his church. He tied the idea of the lack of relaxation, rest, and renewal in our lifestyles to a lack of trust in God. Think about how God points that out in Leviticus.

When you are widowed, it is easy to run scared. I'm about to list some of these fears and the actions we might take to avoid them. Know that these aren't listed to judge—only to help. We've all done these in some way, because no matter how well we have our "act together", we're still flawed deep inside. And especially when the chips are down, it's easy for all of us to try to keep the pain of our solitude away, forgetting that there is a better solution!

Many of us run ourselves ragged trying to avoid something we're afraid of. Does that resonate with you? Maybe being without a husband makes you lonely, and you go and go to avoid moments of solitude.

There is the widow who stores up her treasures to the point of hoarding because she's afraid, without a husband, she might find herself without. Another fear.

Then there is the widow who will spend her money in ways that might lessen the pain of judgment on herself because she no longer has a husband to defend her.

First, I'd like you to notice how our verse in Leviticus ends. *"I am the Lord your God."* In other words, God is telling you—stop trying to do it all. Trust Him. Whatever you're afraid of, you can rest in Him.

So back to spending.

I started out by explaining how my husband appreciated that I kept the house "clean enough" and relaxed. When he was gone, I missed being validated that way. So guess what I did to avoid the scrutiny of perfectionist women around me? Spent money on a housekeeper. Yep—I didn't go to God for my approval and went back to my childhood roots and hired a housekeeper!

It started appropriately. When I found myself with four small boys and no husband, my friends suggested it. I could afford it, the loss was still fresh, and I really needed the help.

But two years later, I still found myself leaning on a paid housekeeper, all the while having this gnawing feeling that I should be trimming that cost from my budget. I would finally announce to her that I'm ready to handle the cleaning on my own, only to find myself stressed out again and picking up the phone to call her.

Finally, I listened to that gnawing conscience God gave me. With college costs and retirement looming ahead, I started to calculate the wasted dollars going "out the window" because something was driving me to live in a perfectly clean home.

Fear.

That's what it was, and as I sat with the Lord

and let Him reveal where I was lacking in courage to trust Him, He showed me.

Bottom line is I hadn't been trusting Christ for my acceptance and approval. Without Tom, I feared if I didn't hire the housekeeper I would lose admiration, and dare I say… companionship of other adult friends at a time when my closest companion, my husband, was gone.

Really looking at it that way made me see how ridiculous it was to keep spending money on a housekeeper. I finally stopped—completely. It's been over a year now, and guess what? My house is clean… enough! I get visitors all the time, and I haven't lost a bit of companionship!

Even without "Alice"!

Can you look honestly at where you might be running yourself ragged, gathering all the grain from the vineyard rather than leaving it, as God tells us in Leviticus? Don't try to do it all. Rest in His love and having to overdo it or overspend.

Blessings, sisters, and may you be strengthened by God's Word!

God in Heaven, Thank You for Your love. Give me rest in that love today. Give me self-control and restraint in my spending when You bring it to mind. Lead me away from loneliness to Your side. Amen

September 10
Where is Home?
By Karen Emberlin

My Father's house has many rooms;
if that were not so, would I have told you
that I am going there to prepare a place for you?
And if I go and prepare a place for you,
I will come back and take you to be with me
that you also may be where I am.
You know the way to the place where I am going.
John 14:2-4 NIV

Home is where you run to when there is confusion outside, a place of comfort, a place to hang your heart, a place to be at peace!

Within two weeks of my husband's unexpected passing, circumstances caused me to leave "our home" and move with family several hundred miles away. Not only was I dealing with the loss of my husband, but also a completely different "lifestyle" in new surroundings. Everyone involved did their best to make me feel comfortable and at home, but it was just not happening. I had such a longing and desire to "just go home" but I didn't know where home was anymore!

During the first eleven months of my journey I continually searched and prayed hoping to find that place I could truly call home – a place to hang my heart – a place to feel at peace. The majority of my time was spent with our daughter and her busy young family. I found that I was not as young as I thought. Keeping up the pace with them was difficult at this stage of my life. Even though I love them dearly, I was not finding the peace and comfort I so longed for. The pieces of the puzzle were just not fitting! I felt as though I was "visiting" and it was time to go home.

Continuing my search, I traveled back to my childhood home spending time with family. During my second visit, God seemed to be telling me this might be the very place I should be. In fact, He wanted me to consider a retirement village!

Even though age wise I may qualify as a senior citizen I really did not think I was old enough to be a resident of such a facility. In my mind, I imagined this being the last place most folks will call home, where you are dependent on others, unable to do things on your own! (I found out later this is not always true.) The more I considered it, the more I realized that even though I would be one of the "youngest" residents, it offered me so much. Due to a few health issues that limit my driving, I could enjoy the benefits of a "community" of services and friendship all under one roof! I had already "let go" of many of my material possessions and now the usual home maintenance responsibilities and care would be included giving me the ability to find my purpose in the Lord!

The Lord opened many doors allowing me to make this possibility a reality. I am now "at home" in a beautiful apartment at a retirement village in my hometown!

In the short time since my arrival I have re-acquainted myself with friends I have not seen in over forty years, traveled to places and done things I never thought possible, yet still have the privacy of my own home. It is not "home" like I shared with my husband for forty-eight years and represents another change on this "unwanted journey", but I have a real peace about being here.

But wait, this is not the end of the story!

In my first weeks of widowhood a friend sensed my longing to go home and put her arms around me saying, "Karen, you do have a home – Heaven is your home". How right she was – even though I have found a new place on this earth to call "home", I know that I will be "finally home" when God calls my name to join Him (and my husband) in heaven!

The following words were written to me after my husband's death

"The Bible assures us that if the Lord created the heavens and earth in a matter of days, His preparation for us in heaven over the past two thousand years will be beyond what we could ever imagine. This is our glorious hope! The prospect of seeing a dearly loved one in the future keeps this hope alive in the present."

How exciting to think about living with my Heavenly Father in a home I will never have to leave, a place of perfect peace, reuniting with loved ones forever!

Lord, continue to be with me and all my dear sisters who have a difficult time finding the right place to call "home". Never let us forget that you have gone to prepare a place for us that will be our final home. Help us to keep our eyes on You until you call us "home". Amen

September 11
I AM Here
By Sarah Rodriguez

Humble yourselves, therefore, under God's mighty hand,
that He may lift you up in due time.
Cast all your anxiety on Him because He cares for you.
1 Peter 5:6-7 NIV

A month after the loss of my husband, a new cell phone was available. Since I was eligible for an upgrade, I decided I would go ahead and make the purchase. I was a little daunted by this task, but I decided to make the leap.

The long-awaited phone finally came in the mail. I spent hours in tears of frustration trying to make sure that all of my old text messages from my husband were backed up so they wouldn't be lost. But after all those hours and tears, I finally realized I had purchased a phone with the wrong amount of storage space. Another trip to the store, another long phone call, more hours later, and a new phone was finally on its way to my house. By the end of this ordeal I had lost a few hours of my life and a few hairs I had pulled from my head.

Why was this all such a big deal, you ask? Because my husband was the one who normally handled all of the electronic issues in our home. He would mention the new phone was coming out and, next thing I knew, I had it in the palm of my hand, with all of the files neatly transferred over. It took me hours upon hours to do something that was so effortless for him. I was so embarrassingly bad at something so simple for him; it frustrated me.

I must admit, out of my frustration, I started to get angry. I was angry my husband wasn't here to help when I needed him. I was angry the littlest things were such a big hassle due to my inadequacy. I was angry I felt so helpless and I was angry I was alone. All in all I was just angry.

In my frustration I cried out to God and told Him how unfair my life was. I told him how hard and lonely it was to do life without my best friend. On and on I went until I had depleted myself of every frustration I felt. At the end of my rant, I felt The Lord say simply "I am here."

He was there the day that my husband left this earth. He was there the day I held my son in my arms knowing his Father would never return. He was there when I laid in bed at night crying lonely tears. And believe it or not He was there when I was frustrated about a silly phone. Whatever I am feeling be it big or small He is there and He cares.

That day I gave every emotion to The Lord. I told Him how I felt and left it at His feet, knowing how deeply He cares about all of my pain. I am sure it won't be the last frustrating situation I endure but one thing is for sure-I know I won't ever face it alone.

Dear God, I thank You that You care about every little thing that concerns me. Thank You that in every fear and frustration, You are there for me. I pray for Your help to get me through the difficult moments ahead, no matter how big or small, and to feel You ever near to me. Amen

September 12
A Place to Ponder
By Sherry Rickard

> *But Mary kept all these things,*
> *and pondered them in her heart.*
>
> *Luke 2:19 NKJV*

What is it like to lose your husband, friend, soul-mate? I have given a lot of thought to this and the best description I can give that others who have not been on our journey can understand follows:

Think about when you plan and take the vacation of a lifetime and it turns out better than you expected. You plan for it, save money, buy tickets, purchase special clothing, pack, etc. Part of the fun of the vacation is the trip to your destination, because once you are packed, you are already on vacation, right?

When you arrive at your destination, you unpack and begin to experience wonderful things. You might take pictures, but you definitely drink in the experience of the vacation and make wonderful memories. At some point, no matter how long your vacation is, you have to think about going home. At some point, you pull out your suitcase and start packing the clothes and souvenirs you know you won't need for the rest of the trip.

Sometimes, during this process you have to go back to your suitcase because you have packed something away that you weren't ready to and that you need. Still, at some point, you have to pack everything away and carry that suitcase to your mode of transportation home.

When you get home, you unpack and as you pull out the dirty clothes to make a pile for laundry, you also have the clothes you wore and were able to wash while away, so they can go straight into their place in your closet, ready to wear. You have to find a place for your souvenirs. You have to take your pictures to be developed and when those come back, wonderful memories flood through you. This unpacking brings both good and not-so-good memories and feelings with it. You often long to return to your vacation, but must stay in your day-to-day world and save money for your next vacation, whenever that may be.

Grieving the loss of my husband has been like what I described above. We had a wonderful life - full of memories. With his death, I had to start packing away parts of that life. It's a slow process, because I have kept my "suitcase" on the floor of my bedroom, unlatched, because I couldn't bear to finish unpacking. Once you totally unpack the vacation is really over. I still go to the "suitcase" and take out the souvenirs and handle them carefully and let them bring a flood of memories to my heart. Wonderful memories.

Each time, I unpack and pack this virtual "suitcase", the sharp pain of my loss lessens. It doesn't hurt as much each time I ponder our life together in my heart. There are memories that I would say should go in the laundry pile - hospital visions, bandages, tears. Then there are the memories that remind me of the breath-taking life we had - his smile, our laughter, shared meals, snuggling. I could go on and on. Those memories are wonderful. My heart has a tug of pain when I think of these things, but then it swells with happiness at having been the recipient of such a wonderful love, even if it ended too soon.

As I prepare to commemorate the third year since his death, I can look back on our wonderful life and not feel the sharp pain I once felt when thinking along these lines. I thank God that He allowed me such a sweet time with my husband and that my memories of that time are still fresh. I can ponder them in my heart and I do.

I encourage you to go to your "suitcase" and allow yourself to experience the wonderful memories of a life well-lived. Ponder these memories in your heart and let the pain be replaced by the sweetness of a wonderful time remembered.

Dear Lord, thank You for the gift of love and for the wonderful memories I hold in my heart of time spent with loved ones. Amen

September 13
A Different Way to Look At Things
By Liz Anne Wright

But we do not want you to be uninformed,
brethren, about those who are asleep,
so that you will not grieve as do the rest who have no hope.
For if we believe that Jesus died and rose again,
even so God will bring with Him
those who have fallen asleep in Jesus.
1 Thessalonians 4:13-14 ESV

Recently at Sunday school, my youngest, age six, unknowingly created a stir among the staff and teachers.

He drew a picture of himself and his dad playing soccer. His dad died when he was seven months old. They never played soccer together.

Now, I appreciate the concern of the teachers. I really do. But...

The staff wanted to make sure I knew right away what he had drawn. When the staff first came to me, I was a bit blind-sided and busy with other things at church. I said, "Thanks for the info," and continued on with my Sunday morning duties.

Looking at the picture the next day, I felt frustration.

Really? You don't understand the grief process any better than to know this is actually a good thing, a normal thing? So what if he imagined playing soccer with his dad? I am sure that all of my boys have thought of doing something with their dad again. The Sunday school lesson was about friendship. I am thankful beyond belief that, even though he did not really know him here on earth, my youngest considers his daddy a friend.

Blessedly, I did not voice those emotions when I was all worked up. I certainly could have "muddied the waters" or caused trouble with my dear friends on the staff.

But now...I am realizing that this is really an *opportunity.*

I was able this week to send to the staff some information I have collected about children and grief...how they process and what it means. I pray they never have to refer to it again, but at least they have it, should they need it. God has put me in the place to educate others on this grief process...what it means and how it works. It is my *job* and my *joy* to share with others how they can truly help the grieving, how to relate to them.

In my opinion, our culture *fears* death too much. While it may be a fear of the unknown, it can be a fear that is crippling, preventing us from dealing with death, the dying…and grief.

I have not shielded my children from the reality of the pain of their loss. It really, really stinks that their dad is not here. Some days still, five and a half years later, are nearly more than I can bear. I know it is the same for them.

My boys deal with the loss in different ways at different times. We have had sleepless nights, where I have one who wants to come snuggle in my bed because of a dream about Dad they cannot seem to forget…or mentally process. They have sad times and mad times, and just lonely times. Just like our grief journey, they have spasms of the grief hit them at different times, especially as they grow and can process more.

And life events happening now affect them. We have been talking about death more in our family recently because a dear family friend just lost her battle with a brain tumor. We went to the memorial service a week ago. I think it is bringing it all up for my sweet little boy. That is totally fine…more opportunities for him to process and ask questions. I know from my own grief that it is an elephant you don't eat all at one time…nobody can.

As we continue to heal from our friend's loss…and process more about dad's…I will continue to watch my boys and answer the questions as they happen. And glory in the fact that both of these people, so important in our lives, are even now in the presence of the Lord, enjoying the things we have only dreamed of.

And, in the meantime, I have a sweet new picture to put on my fridge…of my boy and his daddy playing soccer.

I asked him if he thought there was soccer in Heaven. He said he thought there were better games than that.

Amen and amen!

Dear Father, even as my days on this grief journey lengthen, help me continue to heal. Help me recognize and appropriately act when others are peeling off another "layer" of the grief "onion" to deal with. Help me to guide them into healing and into Your arms. Help me to help others to understand this journey better. Thanks for being a God who cares for me! In Your precious and holy Name, Amen.

September 14
Above the Clouds
By Leah Stirewalt

I look for God everywhere. Truly…I do.

If you consider that the God of the Universe was the Creator of all that we can lay our eyes upon, then we're bound to see His fingerprints everywhere…if we just look for Him.

Early in my grief walk, I didn't have to struggle to see Him. He showed up everywhere for me.

Through people.

Through words.

Through songs.

Through surprises left on my front porch.

Through heart-shaped rocks.

Through flowers.

Through butterflies.

The list is endless. It seemed He knew I needed to see deeper evidence of His presence during those very difficult early weeks and months. We almost had our own little private love language. I sought Him, and I found Him…just like His Word promises (Jeremiah 29:13).

As I continued down Grief Road, however, I sensed God wanting to me to look a little deeper for Him…on my own. He continued to comfort me…He never left me…but, He wanted more than a surface level seeking of Him from me (even as I grieved). So, I spent more time in His Word…I spent longer time in prayer. I continued to find Him.

Many months later, I found I was doing pretty well "on my own". Or – so I thought. Allow me to be a little transparent, if you will.

A great healing from the agony of grief had taken root, and as it did, my reliance on Him didn't go away, but it certainly decreased a little. I started carrying some of my own battles again. I even began taking credit for some minor victories. Yes. I admit it. For the first time during this widowhood journey, I was a bit too self-reliant. But God…

He didn't allow that to linger too long. I'm so thankful for that. It wasn't long before I returned to His lap, crying tears of repentance for neglecting some of our time together, for not being as diligent as I had been, and for settling for less of Him. His forgiveness and mercy washed all over me, and we began walking hand-in-hand again.

Recently I had the opportunity to fly out-of-state for a quick weekend trip. As the plane began its descent into my final destination, I noticed the beautiful sunset from above the clouds. I simply stared, knowing that God wanted me to see something else from this viewpoint. I just couldn't take my eyes off of it. It was absolutely stunning. And…to think, I would have never seen this view of the sunset from underneath the clouds.

"What is it, Lord?" I asked him. "What is it that you want me to see?"

Daughter, never forget this view. When the times come, as they have this past year through the grief of your beloved Chris' death, when you don't understand My ways…when you don't understand My perspective…when you just want answers to things that don't make sense…remember this view. Allow it to remind you that most of the time, you can't see the things that I see. You can't understand My ways, because they are out of your scope of understanding. Your perspective of life is limited by your "under the clouds" viewpoint. Every now and then, I may give you a glimpse above the clouds. But, trust that just because you can't always see it…the sun still sets. Just because you can't always see evidences of My presence, I'm always with you. Just because life makes no sense at times and seems very, very unfair – I'm still sovereign, I still have you in the palm of My hand, and I love you with an everlasting love.

Thank you Father for that beautiful "above the clouds" glimpse of your setting sun and the sweet, teachable moment you gave your daughter. I love you, Abba!

September 15
Thou Changest Not
By Nancy Howell

I the LORD do not change.
Malachi 3:6 NCV

Life is full of changes. Maybe that's the understatement of the year, especially considering the audience reading this. Those of us who have lost loved ones, beloved spouses, know this all too well. Life is not static, but constantly in flux and in motion.

What you once thought would last a lifetime ended way too soon.

Circumstances beyond your control--accidents, sickness, cancer, heart attack, infection after surgery--changed your perfect world in an instance. You are alone, in a daze, struggling to make sense of your situation. You feel like there's a piece missing from your body, an integral one that you need to keep going.

Everything that you know and love has changed.

Or has it?

One of my late husband's favorite hymns is "Great is thy Faithfulness" by Thomas Chisolm. The beautiful words are based on the passage from Lamentations:

The steadfast love of the Lord never ceases,
his mercies never come to an end;
they are new every morning;
great is your faithfulness.
Lamentations 3:22-23 NRSV

But my favorite phrase of that hymn? "Thou changest not, Thy compassions they fail not"

I lost the love of my life, but "Thou changest not."

I have so much now on my plate, so many more responsibilities as a single woman, but "Thou changest not."

My world has been turned upside down, but "Thou changest not."

Happiness and purpose in my life seem oh-so-far away, but "Thou changest not."

In all that flux, constant change, chaos of your world, God doesn't change.

He is the one and only constant in your life.

I needed reminding of this simple fact just this week. Dealing with household repairs and remodels, the sad reality set in--I was changing "our" house, remodeling "our" bathrooms, repainting "our" bedroom. Life had moved on, and I had moved with it.

Down came the prints and portraits from the bedroom walls, holes were spackled and filled. The blank walls were repainted a soft yellow. It wasn't "our" room anymore, but solely "mine."

As I took stock of which items to re-display on the walls, the past year replayed through my mind. In all of the changes in my world, God was there. **He didn't change.**

And though I have moved on in many respects, I will never forget the quarter century of life and laughs and love I was lucky enough to have with my spouse.

In whatever phase of change you find yourself

in today, remember you are never alone. Whether you are newly widowed, struggling with chaos and loneliness, or just beginning to find a new "normal", God has a plan. He has a glorious plan for you, just for you, wherever you are in your journey.

Never ever forget--His mercies are new each morning, His compassion never fails, He is faithful, and He doesn't change.

Heavenly Father, Thank You for never changing, for being the great "I AM", the One constant in a world full of confusion and chaos. Keep reminding me of my purpose. I want to discover the plans that You have for me. Help me be patient for grief is such a complex difficult process. I want to come through the grief stronger, more closely aligned with Your will, and ready for whatever the future holds. Thou changest not....hallelujah! Amen

September 16
The 16th
By Erika Graham

> *This is the day The Lord has made,*
> *we will rejoice and be glad in it.*
> *Psalm 118:24 NLT*

The sixteenth was the most joyous day around

my house for many years. September sixteen was my husband's birthday, we met on October sixteen, and so we chose August sixteen as our wedding day. My reasoning was he never forgot his birthday or the day we met, so our anniversary would be equally as easy to remember. We celebrated the sixteenth many times over. It was our day!

Then my husband's death changed all that. He went to heaven on June sixteenth, and it seemed to go from a joyous day to a cursed day for me. Each month, I dreaded and loathed it. Sixteen was a number that had betrayed me. I marked it off on the calendar the first year every month, one month ago, two months ago, three months ago, four months ago.... For a long time I had to begrudgingly acknowledge the sixteenth and hated how it contained a tangible reminder of all I lost.

Now, I know God knows.

I also know because, without hesitation, I said I wanted the number sixteen as my shirt number for a women's basketball league. I run around with sixteen plastered on my back as I play every Sunday night.

But wait...what am I thinking? The sixteenth became cursed, right?

I lead with my heart, and my heart has Christ. In what seems like an impulsive choice with my basketball team and an odd coincidence with this ministry, I realize it's entirely the LORD. When asked what number I'd like, my mouth blurted out the number sixteen from my heart, before my brain got in the way. When asked if the schedule looked good, I confirmed without even noticing the date was the sixteenth for the next few months.

God is here and He knows.

God gave me the gift of joyous celebrations on the sixteenth for so many years. Satan tried to claim sixteen for himself through my husband's suicide. But, God knew that someday having all these events fall on the same day would somehow help me go back and remember and also help me move forward. He knew way back then that now I'd be writing about my journey on the sixteenth of the month, and that I'd be running around every Sunday joyously on the basketball court with sixteen on my back. He knew that what Satan tried to steal, He'd claim and use for His honor and glory and my good.

It's amazing to see my life through this date three and a half years later. It's still a whopper of a few months that hit me almost consecutively: June 16, August 16, September 16, and October 16. Of course, three of these dates no longer carry the joy they once did because of the fourth one. But, they no longer feel like they betrayed me either. They are just days, my days, days The Lord made.

The sixteenth has been claimed by God as my day. Now it's my turn to find ways to rejoice and be glad in it. Sometimes that's easy and sometimes that's hard. But it's possible because I have Christ and I can trust Him. I've seen Him work to heal me and make sixteen all mine.

Heavenly Father, I have peace in Your words that this day is the day You made for me. I embrace it, and I ask that You continue to use me to bring honor and glory to You as I share my story. I pray that You help me move my day from pain and hurt to a place of peace, as I move forward and see it in a new light. In your matchless name, Amen.

September 17
Crying Out in the Battle
By Elizabeth Dyer

They cried out to Him during the battle.
He answered their prayers, because they trusted in Him.
1 Chronicles 5:20b NIV

Have you felt like you are in a battle? A battle for your soul? For your future? For your joy? For your security? Maybe for your family?

I know I have felt like I have been in battles over my lifetime. There was the battle for my sanity while I lived abroad after college, not knowing much of the language or having friends. I wasn't able to sit and play the piano like I was used to when I needed to relax. I felt like I could have easily lost my sanity but I was able to cry out to God there in a distant land without the help of my family or home church. I had to trust God all on my own. He gave me a wonderful friend that was more than I asked for. He gave me experiences that helped to mature my personality and faith.

Many couples feel like they are in a battle for their marriages. You may have been one of those. You had to trust that God heard your prayers, even when things may not have improved.

After your husband passed away, you began a battle for your future and your joy. Your security and your family. Do you remember the first few hours? You had to remind yourself to breathe. You were not sure you should be left in charge of those small children. Your battle was beginning and you may not have been ready for it.

Trust.

Sometimes that word brings comfort. Sometimes fear.

"Because they trusted in Him."

You had to trust that God was hearing your prayers. You had to trust that God knew what was going on. That God, all-loving and all-powerful, had a plan that included this most painful experience.

Do you recall the trust it took at the very beginning of your widow journey? Do you recall specific events when trust was all you had?

I had to battle for my family. I was not going to allow Satan to drag us into deep pits of depression. We were sad, yes, very sad. We lost our strong male influence. How in the world was I capable of leading these children? I had to consciously decide that Trust in God was the way we were going to fight this battle for joy.

Recently I have again felt the fears during a battle. My security is at risk. Where will I find employment when I have basically been home raising children for nearly twenty years? Insurance. Retirement. Investments. All these areas pull at me and beg for me to trust them. I have to battle those security issues by fully trusting God with my future. Fully.

Today, what battle are you fighting? Trust in God, the author and perfecter of our faith (Hebrews 12:2). Go back to Hebrews chapter 11, often called the Faith Hall of Fame. Look at all the battles that those individuals fought while trusting God for the outcome. We have the advantage of His Word to guide us. Let's use it!

Father God, thank You for the faith You have authored in my life. Faith that trusts in You during my difficult battles. Thank You for pushing me and molding me into the woman of faith You need for furthering Your Kingdom. Remind me today how far I have come on my journey and how You have upheld me with Your Mighty Hands. Amen

September 18
No More Shame
By Leah Stirewalt

I had been on a bit of a hiatus since my husband's suicidal death…a public speaking hiatus, that is. I have no problem sharing the story of how God miraculously healed me following my husband's death; however I haven't really pushed to do so either. I waited on Him to open that door when He felt I was ready.

It just so happened…He opened the door, when I had the opportunity to share at a women's event with a group of nearly two thousand women. I was so nervous, because honestly, I was afraid I would lose composure and start sobbing on stage. But God…God allowed the tears to form but not simply take over. His peace literally surrounded me like a cloud the moment I stepped on the stage. I knew His Presence was abundantly there that evening.

However, I wasn't prepared for what came later in the evening. I had the pleasure of talking with several women, hearing their stories-stories of tragedy resulting from a loved one's suicide. My eyes welled up with tears again. I saw the pain – often redemptive – cross their faces. It was the tears…the pain…the stories that surprised me. It was the fact that most have seldom spoken of their pain because of the shame they've been carrying.

I know that feeling…all too well. I just wasn't prepared to see so many other precious women experiencing that type of guilt and shame as well.

After my husband's death, I experienced a temporary season of shame. While suicide can easily usher in unwanted and unmerited shame, I've also learned that shame all-too-often accompanies any type of death of a spouse. But why?

Far too often, we feel we should have done something. If I had only done this or that…if I had only taken him to the hospital sooner…if only I had listened better when he shared his burdens about work…if only I had told him I loved him one last time. On and on the "if onlys" go. On and on the "what ifs" and the "shoulda couldas" continue.

I honestly had to learn the hard way that shame will take me nowhere except deeper into my pit of grief. As a believer, I also have to trust in the truths from God's Word.

Romans 8:1-2 promises us… *Therefore, there is now no condemnation for those who are in Christ Jesus, because through Christ Jesus the law of the Spirit of life set me free from the law of sin and death. (NIV)*

I truly believe the enemy throws the dart of shame our way to try to render us useless for kingdom work. And what better time than when we're already lower than low while grieving. However…God has another plan. Are we willing to trust Him with it?

His plan is to heal!

His plan is to rescue!

His plan is to deliver!

His plan is to restore!

His plan is to provide divine peace!

His plan is to strengthen!

His plan is to comfort so that we can comfort others!

His plan is to redeem our pain!

Friends – we have so many other women that will come behind us seeking refuge, seeking peace, seeking restoration, seeking hope. God wants to use you! Will you let Him? Tell the enemy to back off…cling to the promises in God's Word…and watch God heal you beyond belief. While it may not look like it's ever going to come, just trust Him. He's reaching for YOU. He wants to rescue YOU. And, He promises to restore YOU.

So with you: Now is your time of grief, but I will see you again and you will rejoice, and no one will take away your joy.
John 16:22 NIV

Lord God, thank You healing does come. Use me to help other women seek refuge, peace, restoration, and hope. Remind me that shame is not from You but from the Enemy, Satan. Restore me as I cling to Your promises. Amen

September 19
Consider That Terrible Struggle, Joy?
By Kit Hinkle

Consider it pure joy, my brothers,
whenever you face trials of many kinds.
James 1:2 NIV

So many times our articles are focused on encouragement. We share with you how to move forward, how to put your trust in the Lord, and how to take the lemons that widowhood has left for you and make lemonade—and maybe even something better than lemonade. Maybe even a pineapple lemon-drop smoothie!

But I can remember moments, especially in that first year of widowhood, when that advice was the last thing I wanted to hear. Recently I chatted with a widow who spent her first holiday alone after losing her husband. She wondered if our writing team ever got angry with God, or if we were just filled with God's euphoria all the time? Her comment rang out with bitterness in this brief conversation.

His love for me is of no comfort to me right now because it seems ... He gets to do whatever it is He wants with my life and I am still supposed to take comfort in His love.

She recognized this anger will pass, but she was fed up with encouragement when she is just not ready for it—not just yet. She just wanted to be mad.

Truth is, sisters, yes, each one of us had and continues to have our moments when we cry out in pain, in anger, in self-pity.

My moments like this came, at first, in waves—like a roller coaster. One moment I'd feel this surreal peace, like God had me totally in His grip, and the next moment the entire loss would come crashing in on me like a tidal wave. The night my husband died, I felt a surreal lifting from the Lord—like, even though I lost the best friend and love of my life, Someone was supernaturally holding me, cradling me, carrying me. But just minutes later, I found myself looking at his chair in the living room in disbelief, remembering how earlier that day he sat there, grinning at me. "He was just here," I thought. I found myself grabbing at the empty space where he sat with my fist, over and over, until I exploded in tears.

And then on that first Christmas without him, I found myself too busy with my four boys to get to that miserably lonely point. Friends and family surrounded me, and I still felt that glow of being loved by my husband—still felt married. But just two days later, as I finally cleaned out his office, turning paper after paper over, sorting, what memory to toss, what memory to savor. I found little notes I had written to him, just months before, weighing the merits of which vacation we'd take in the fall. Little did I know as I had scribbled those thoughts, he'd be gone before we could ever take that vacation. I sobbed my eyes out, wondering if it will ever be possible to stop? Nothing would dull the pain, sleep fled from me, and I became determined to finish the painful sorting job even as the sun started to climb over the horizon.

At the first year anniversary of his death, friends and family gathered to help the boys and me celebrate the memory of Tom Hinkle with a joyful celebration. The boys enjoyed it—it was beautifully perfect.

But that same moment, as dozens smiled and prayed and encouraged with words, cards, letters, and mementos, I was dying inside. I wanted everyone to just go away. I wanted to be alone. I hated the attention—I hated that all I had was a memory to celebrate, not the husband that cradled me in his arms night after night. I left those dozens of cards people gave me unopened. Tucked them away in a box, still unopened after many years. I just wanted to forget that horrible night where we had to celebrate the memory of someone I wanted to spend the rest of my life with.

If you're angry, you're probably not really blaming God and thinking He's laughing at you and hurling death into your life to watch you squirm. But you're still angry at Him.

And if you're still angry at Him, you're probably mad because you know He's all-powerful, and He could have stopped it. He could have stopped the car wreck, or the heart attack or the cancer cells. But He didn't. And now you have to be happy with the comfort He gives you? Arrrgh!!!

So why didn't I cave to those feelings, and why won't you?

Because you have to believe, somewhere deep within you, that there is a purpose to allowing pain in our lives. You're angry, sad, lonely. And you might stay that way, but if you get past that, you begin look around and really notice God more. You're comforted by Him and suddenly you see Him like you've never seen Him before.

But I encourage you—look around while

you're in that place. You begin seeing the beauty of this road. And that beauty, my sisters, is the euphoria that you read about here.

September 20
Misunderstood
By Rene Zonner

Before a word is on my tongue: you, Lord, know it completely.
Psalm 139:4 NIV

Some days I feel like beating my head against a wall.

Friends and family just don't get what I'm trying to say.

It feels like I'm speaking a foreign language.

I am. It's called Widowhood.

Since becoming a "citizen" of the "state of widowhood", I have learned that those who aren't on this journey with me often misunderstand my words and actions. Most of the time they are trying to understand. Friends and family do their best to decipher what I'm saying. Unless, however, they also speak "widow", they just won't get it.

Losing a spouse has changed my perspective on everything. What I say, what I do, what I think…it's all filtered through grief now. Material possessions mean so much less than they ever did before because I had to sort through every piece of my husband's belongings. It drove the point home that we take nothing with us when we leave this life. My husband died when I was not at home, and unreachable, so now I carry my cellphone with me everywhere I go and feel anxiety if I can't be contacted by loved ones. I am much more vocal in sharing my thoughts and opinions because the reality that we aren't guaranteed tomorrow is in my face all the time.

Sure, others have suffered loss too, and life is now filtered through grief for them. But the loss of a friend, the loss of a parent or a child is not the same as the loss of a spouse. I'm not saying my grief is worse or more important...just different. I've suffered a terrible loss in my life, but I would still struggle to understand what it would be like for the person who lost a child.

Even other widows sometimes misunderstand me. See, in the "language" of widowhood there are lots of "dialects". There are widows who lost husbands suddenly like me, but then there are those who had to suffer through a long illness. Those who lost husbands early in their life together and those who had more time. Widows who were left financially secure and those who are struggling. We can never truly understand another's language, and they can never truly understand ours.

So I find myself asking, "Is there anyone who gets me?"

Thankfully, the answer is yes!

We are told in the Bible that God knows us better than we know ourselves. He gets it. He understands why I say, do and think the things I do. I don't have to explain myself to Him. He created me, He knit me in my mother's womb. He knows the number of hairs on my head. I can just rest in his intimate knowledge of me. In His arms I am no longer misunderstood and I am not merely understood…I am known.

There was a time when I had some people take offense at something I said about my late husband and about our life together. They were hurt by my words, and that truly pained me. Because they could have been listening from the perspective of someone who lost a child, a brother, a cousin, or other close loved one, they couldn't understand the words I spoke as someone who lost her spouse. My motives were questioned, the love I had for my husband doubted, and my faith scrutinized. I found myself extremely discouraged because I was so misunderstood. I cried out to God, begging for Someone to know my heart.

God answered. He soothed my heart and reminded me that ultimately the only person who needs to understand me is Him. I allowed the Holy Spirit to examine my heart and my motives and, in doing so, found peace. I allowed the words of the Psalm 139 to soothe me and comfort me. He knew just what words I needed to hear because He created me.

Friends, if it hasn't happened already, there is going to be a time when you are misunderstood. Your heart may be called into question. It will be tempting to try and explain yourself or justify your actions to others. You may be hurt and tempted to speak harshly to those who aren't walking your walk. But when that occurs, I encourage you to go first to God. Ask Him to examine your heart and, if you have peace with your words or actions, then find your comfort in being known by the God of the universe. Once that knowledge truly sinks in, it becomes so much easier to respond in love to those who may criticize.

Father, thank You for the knowledge that You understand me in ways that no one else ever can. There will be people in my life who won't get why I say or do the things I do. There will be times when I feel so misunderstood. Remind me that You know me so intimately because You created me. Lord, give me patience with those who are not walking my walk and may misunderstand me. Holy Spirit, reveal to me times when I may need to soften my words and those times when I need to stay true to what I believe. Thank You again, Precious Lord, for being my Rock and my Salvation. Amen

September 21
Un-Taken... And Re-Taken
By Liz Anne Wright

> *I have loved you with an everlasting love;*
> *I have drawn you with unfailing kindness.*
> *I will build you up again,*
> *and you, Virgin Israel, will be rebuilt.*
> *Again you will take up your timbrels*
> *and go out to dance with the joyful.*
> *Jeremiah 31:3b-4 NIV*

"When did you take your wedding rings off?"
Ah, the $64,000 question.
I thought back to my own decision, so I knew what to tell this dear friend who had just lost his wife.
Right after my husband died, I had no thought to taking off my rings, was not sure I would

ever take them off. They were my link to *him*, a visible reminder that he had been here...and married to me.

Soon after, though, I began to have other thoughts...remarrying someday, having to explain time after time that I was not still married when asked questions about my husband.

A dear friend told me the decision was mine alone, but perhaps I should move my rings to the other hand as an intermediate step. If that worked, I could easily remove them for good. If not, I could just as easily slip them back on to the other hand.

That seemed like a good decision, so I tried it. The rings felt a little strange on the other hand, but I left them there.

For about two weeks.

During that time, another thought struck me. *I did not want to live just as Keith's widow.*

One day, I knew I wanted to emerge as more than Keith's widow...to again become *Liz*...just Liz. I wasn't there yet, but I knew that I wanted to be.

For me, that made the decision about my rings easy.

About three months after Keith died, I took them off for good. I was almost afraid not to, for fear I might be stuck in that world of *the Widow Wright* instead of the world of *Liz*.

For me, it was the right decision.

Others I know have made different decisions, weighing in on the side of not wanting to date again, or not wanting to look like an example of divorce (just another failed marriage).

For a long time, I wore no rings. Any rings seemed a painful reminder of what I had taken off...and lost. I stored them all in my jewelry box, along with my rings from Keith, for another day.

Today, I wear a couple of new rings. They both contain Bible verses: the Lord's Prayer and Jeremiah 29:11.

They speak to me about a different kind of pledge or symbol of the "new" Liz. They speak of my devotion to my Heavenly Bridegroom.

I was a believer before Keith died. I have grown in leaps and bounds in my faith since then...out of necessity.

The most important thing is that the commitment God has made to me is even stronger than the one that Keith made to me. He has promised to always, always, *always* be there...through thick and thin, in sickness and in health. Sound familiar?

But there is a difference in His commitment and the one that Keith made to me...He will be there not until death do us part, but *especially after that...into eternity*. Praise Him for that!

I may no longer be "taken" in the sense that I was when Keith was here, but I am still "taken" by a Savior Who gave His life for me.

Has a nice ring to it, doesn't it?

Dear Father, thank You for Your incredible, unending, unwavering love. Thank You for the man I had in my life and the wonderful love that we shared. Thank You for caring for me since then, and promising to care for me every day for forever. That gives me the strength to get through whatever is to come, knowing that You are there with me. In Jesus' name I pray, Amen.

September 22

Why Now? What If?
By Karen Emberlin

*Your eyes saw my unformed body;
all the days ordained for me were written in your book
before one of them came to be.*
                                        Psalm 139:16 NIV

*A person's days are determined;
you have decreed the number of his months
and have set limits he cannot exceed.*
                                        Job 14:5 NIV

Have you ever asked, "Why, Lord, did you take my husband now?" or "Could I have done something to prevent his passing?"

These two questions are clearly etched in my mind, they've been there for many months. My seemingly-healthy husband and I had no reason to believe anything serious was on the horizon. We spent New Year's Day together with no signs of any problems. We retired for the night. I, unfortunately, could not get comfortable, ending up tossing and turning.

Around two a.m. my husband and I agreed on my relocating to a recliner for the remainder of the night. I would be more comfy, and hopefully he would get some rest. Sleep finally came to me there in my chair. Mere words will never be able to completely describe my shock to find, upon awaking at eight a.m., that he had passed away at some point in his sleep!

Even though I have been told time and time again that remaining next to him in our bed all night wouldn't have changed the sad outcome, I still wonder "what if" and "why". I most likely always will. It's human nature.

I do know this: the Lord has been with me every day of this "journey" which began that sad morning sixteen months ago. Without a doubt He has given me strength to move forward. I have the promise and hope that I will see my husband again. However......the "why" and "what if" questions and thoughts still lurk in the back of my mind--no matter how much I want them to leave.

Last week-end I attended a retreat with eight ladies from a Bible study group of which I am a member.

One of our discussion subjects was "Grief." It focused on the key verse *Psalm 139:16, Your eyes saw my unformed body; all the days ordained for me were written in your book before one of them came to be. NIV*

I have read this verse countless times. But this time, it was like God turned on a light bulb in my soul, helping me understand that in no circumstance can we either add or take from the days which are ordained for each of us (my husband)! It was my beloved spouse's time to go to heaven. I could not have done anything to prevent it.

But even with this new understanding, my feelings of grief are not gone. I've made a lot of progress, but it will take more time, more tears, copious prayers, and letting go of the search for answers to these "why" and "what if" questions. To continue my healing process, I must choose to look at what plans the Lord has in store for me with a renewed perspective.

I anxiously await the time when my deep

sense of loneliness will lessen, when guilt-free laughter returns to my life, and I can look forward with great anticipation to the future God has planned for me.

Our lives are like a piece of rich beautiful tapestry woven by the Lord. We cannot choose the colors and often times He weaves sorrow into the pattern. In my foolish pride I sometimes forget He sees the upper side, and I, only the underside.

In time God will unroll the finished textile, explaining the reason dark threads of sadness and sorrow are as necessary as the threads of gold and silver in the pattern He has woven. I'd like to think that the sadness and sorrow, seen in the dark stitching, adds depth and a subtle beauty, in contrast to the bright and sunny threads. God knows we have to experience both.

Lord, please help me replace my questions of "why" and "what if" with truth from Your Word. I pray Your presence will help me see good can come and will come in You and through You. You are such an awesome God. I love you! Amen

September 23
All Eyes Are Not On You
By Kit Hinkle

Be still, and know that I am God: I will be exalted among the heathen, I will be exalted in the earth.
Psalm 46:10 KJV

"Please pray for me to be joyous. I want to be a light to people around me."

The words of my precious friend came at a moment of desperation when she so felt the pressure of having to be "the good Christian woman" handling her time of sorrow with God given grace. All the while, she felt lost in her sadness.

Take pause, show tears

Know it's okay to grieve and have tears. Be soft in your vulnerabilities. In seeing us in our weakness, others learn they're not alone in their pain.

To be a light to others, we need to also let others observe us in pain, then let them see us turn our pain into boldness and energy to move forward. If we only show the positive side of grief, we could slip into a pattern of pretending. The "good Christian woman" who handles her grief with no vulnerability seems too high up on a pedestal—an example too perfect to be of any use by others. The times people have seen me spill tears over Tom makes their witness of my pinnacles of joy and bold steps forward more real as God's light in their lives.

It's hard to show vulnerability

When the loss was fresh, I felt so much attention on me. The way people fussed over me both warmed me and made me feel awkward. I didn't want them to stop because I didn't want to be alone. At the same time, I felt pitying eyes constantly watching me through my ups and downs. The attention made me self-conscious over my actions.

At times my actions were bold and strong and full of God's joy. God was carrying me and I knew my strength was real and in Him. In those moments I worried people would think I didn't miss my husband enough. I worried they would think my God-filled joy disrespectful to someone deceased. Other times I cried—especially in those first few years. I would then worry over what others thought of my tears, embarrassed to be the object of everyone's sympathy.

Don't put pressure on yourself

Don't fret over what others think of your grieving.

Women are so naturally wired to worry about relationships and people around us. Sometimes, it's a relief to remember that people aren't always focused on exactly what we are doing or what our reactions and behaviors are.

Really, everyone is so busy with their lives— just reassuring them how grieving naturally involves a mix of tears and triumphs is the best way to handle what feels like the glare of people noticing us in our grief.

Still yourself

I was only able to be a light when I stopped my worry over what they thought of me. I purposefully stilled the thoughts, as the Psalmist wrote God asks us to do. "Be still and know that I am God." I had to stop looking around me for approval and accept only the watchful eyes of the Father.

Rest in Him as the Psalmist suggests. People expect neither unnatural joy nor gnashing of teeth during our grief. Often we presume people are watching when really, we have the freedom to take time to just experience our sadness. Just acknowledging our pain helps us heal and move on.

Dear Lord, give me the ability to accept the loss that's been presented in my life and a stillness in my heart that protects me from feeling observed and exposed. Help me to see the attention given from those around me not through our flesh of self-absorbed anxieties. People care and love me. Help me to accept that love and read nothing more into it. Give me the freedom to grieve the way You ask me to and not feel pressured to express myself the way I think others expect my grief to be expressed. In Jesus' Name, Amen.

September 24
Dearly Loved
By Sheryl Pepple

Therefore, as God's chosen people, holy and dearly loved,
clothe yourselves with compassion, kindness, humility,
gentleness and patience.
Bear with each other and forgive whatever grievances
you may have against one another.
Forgive as the Lord forgave you.
And over all these virtues put on love,
which binds them all together in perfect unity.
Colossians 3:12-13 NIV

His Word is His love letter to us. Sometimes we are in so much pain, it is hard to remember that He is there. He is. Take some time today to spend with Him, pour out your heart to Him. He will answer.

Below is a copy of my letter to God, written

just thirteen days after my husband's death. I poured out my heart to God, and He was there. On that day and many days since, He has reminded me that I am holy and dearly loved.

Dear Heavenly Father,

I sit before you today as your child with a broken heart…but all the pieces are yours. As much as I love my husband, miss him and struggle with this unbearable pain- I love You more than anything or anyone. You gave me that gift, a heart that loves You through all things. As much as my mind struggles with the losses I have experienced-I love You more. As much as I struggle with wanting to be brought home and delivered from this world, this pain, I love You more. Your Word tells me in Colossians 3:12, as God's chosen people (which I am), I am holy and dearly loved. Lord, I am struggling with this pain but I know two things: 1) You are sovereign over everything and everyone and 2) You are good. I thank You for that wisdom and the strength that comes from Your truth. I feel broken and of no value but I know that You live in me and that You will continue to fulfill Your purposes through me. My life is not my own, it is Yours. It was bought at a price and now, through my husband's death, I have a better appreciation of the price that was paid. Lord, there is so much I don't understand but I know Your will is perfect, pleasing and acceptable. I know that I am not to lean on my own understanding. Lord, I hurt, I am broken, but I am Your chosen one. I am holy and dearly loved.

I pray today you will pour out your heart to God and let Him comfort you as only He can. I pray you will be reminded that you are Holy and Dearly Loved!

If you are uncertain if you are His chosen one,

then cry out to Him and ask Him to be Lord of your life. He will answer.

For God so loved the world
that he gave his one and only Son,
that whoever believes in him
shall not perish but have eternal life.
John 3:16 NIV

September 25
Standing Firm
By Liz Anne Wright

Now fear the Lord and serve Him with all faithfulness.
Throw away the gods your ancestors worshiped beyond the
Euphrates River and in Egypt, and serve the Lord.
But if serving the Lord seems undesirable to you,
then choose for yourselves this day whom you will serve,
whether the gods your ancestors served beyond the Euphrates,
or the gods of the Amorites, in whose land you are living.
But as for me and my household, we will serve the Lord.
Joshua 24:14-15 NIV

My sweet friend returned to church for the first time since her husband passed. As you know, that takes courage. Somehow, where we worship the Lord, where we sat with our husbands and open hearts to the Lord, can often be the rawest of wounds.

One of the hard parts of returning to church

is choosing where to sit. Do you sit where you always did with him, or do you find a new place? There is no wrong answer to this question. I have had friends make both choices. Here is how I made my decision.

When our church built its new building twelve years ago, we put scriptures all over the floor in permanent marker just before they laid the carpet. The idea was to be a reminder that we are standing on the Word of God. Neat tradition! My husband wanted to put the Joshua scripture above on the floor under where we sat. It was his life verse. Being creatures of habit, especially him, we planned to sit in the new building in the same place where we had always sat in the rental facility.

He carefully viewed where the pulpit would be, marked off about where our chairs would be once the sanctuary was finished, and then wrote the scripture right there. It was actually a little amusing to watch. But the sentiment was very sweet, the devotion very real. He wanted his family to follow the Lord. Period.

If we read the Scriptures about Joshua, we see the godly man he was, and the strength in the Lord by which he led his family. He definitely talked the talk *and* walked the walk. I think there is no better statement that can be made of a child of God.

My sweet husband was the same kind of man. His funeral was packed with people whom I knew, and many I did not know, who all said similar things about his character. What a tremendous testimony to who he was!

And what a legacy to leave for me and the boys! His strong leadership of our family allowed us to grieve his loss, but with hope; to accept gracefully his death, just as he accepted his illness; and to *put God first*, no matter what.

We are a changed family by losing Keith. But…we are still a family seeking after God's will. We are a family who has Christ as the cornerstone of our home and of our lives. That did not change when we lost Keith.

Today, years later, as I still sit in the same spot, I take great comfort in the fact that my husband's words are still right below my feet, that I am standing firm of them. My aim is to raise my sons to be strong men of God like their father, men who not only talk the talk but also walk the walk. I happily stand firm in Him who gave His life for me. It is not always easy, but it is *always* worth it.

We all have to make a lot of choices in this new life, dear sisters. Where you choose to sit in church is but one. I pray that as you face the myriad of choices of this new and unexpected path, you continue to lean on the Lord. He is the One who can help you to stand firm.

Dear Father, when I am broken before You in my grief, help me stay on Your path. Help me stand firm in You, leaning on Your Word as my guide for life. Help me make the choices, both big and small, You would have me make. Help me see You in the place of leadership. In Your Son's Name, Amen.

September 26
Full Circle
By Leah Stirewalt

As I read her email, I honestly thought it was some sort of spam message sent under my friend's name. Certainly this couldn't be real. I re-read it. The words simply stunned me. She simply said, "I really, really need you to pray for me. My husband died yesterday."

Before going any further, I need to give you a little background here. I "met" my friend via Facebook when she read a post from a mutual friend about my "missing" husband who was later discovered, having been welcomed into the arms of Jesus. She has been caring for me for months through cards, a Christmas ornament, and most especially TONS of prayer! While we have never officially met, we got to "know" each other first through Facebook and then through my grief journey I subsequently blogged about.

This friend's physically and mentally handicapped adult son entered the hospital very sick recently. He has cerebral palsy and had developed a pretty severe case of pneumonia. My friend had been faithful to keep a group of us up-to-date on her son and how we could pray for him. So, when I got that message, I - at first - thought it would be an update on her son. Instead, the shocking words informed me that she had just said goodbye to her precious husband. I cried for her. I remember - all too well - the pain of those initial days of grief following the death of a spouse.

On that first day, I had no idea the journey I was about to embark upon, but I was blessed with love from other widows from all over the world that I had never met. They heard "my story", and they flooded me with comfort. I never dreamed that one day I'd be in a position to offer comfort back to another, but God has brought me to that very place. I have come full circle.

While on Grief Road, I have encountered many other widows. I have heard countless stories - many similar to my own. Many were widowed before me. Some were directed to my website following their own encounter with widowhood. However, this particular friend is the only one (to my knowledge) that has walked Grief Road alongside me from my first day and is now experiencing much of the same pain having just joined our beloved sisterhood of widows. She had watched my walk down this path and has now stepped on the path with me.

I prayed, *Lord, please let me live out Second Corinthians chapter one. Please help me to comfort her with the comfort I've received from You and from those You've sent to me. Please send her an entourage of people to support her during this difficult first year, especially.*

I feel so inadequate, at times, but it's not about my abilities. God doesn't call the equipped; He equips the called! I went to visit my friend, the day after her husband's memorial service. I visited with her and her precious son in the hospital. We hugged, we talked, we prayed.

And, she shared this with me: "When I first heard that your husband was missing and then later learned that he had been found in the arms of Jesus, my heart broke for you. I have been drawn to pray for you in ways that I really didn't understand. I never knew you, but the Lord kept drawing me to you. Now...I know. He was preparing me for the widow's journey too. He knew that I would need you."

WOW!

As tears filled my eyes, I silently praised God.

Thank You, Father, for not letting my husband's suicide be in vain. Thank You for bringing beauty from ashes. Thank you for bringing me full circle!

My sweet sisters...you never know the fruit that God will bring from your tragedy. But, it's ALL for His Glory! May each of us strive to walk out our difficult days with our eyes toward Heaven and our hearts toward those grieving around us. May we be more sensitive to the pain of others. May we be "Jesus with skin on" to those He places in our circles of influence.

Praise be to the God and Father of our Lord Jesus Christ, the Father of compassion and the God of all comfort, who comforts us in all our troubles, so that we can comfort those in any trouble with the comfort we ourselves have received from God. For just as the sufferings of Christ flow over into our lives, so also through Christ our comfort overflows.

2 Corinthians 1:3-5 NIV

September 27
1084 Days
By Sherry Rickard

It has been 1,084 days since the love of my life went Home to live with Jesus. We had the kind of relationship (and were blessed with jobs) that we talked via cell phone throughout the day and then checked in on our way home from work to plan for the evening. We were content in each other's company. Both of us were grounded in Christ and just really liked each other.

Now, I don't want you to think of what I have described above as a love story movie-of-the-week; we were real people and we had our real moments. My husband was a plumber and he would wait for me to get in the shower and then turn off the hot water heater and go to work. Then he'd call later to see how my day was going. I would throw ice cubes over the shower curtain rod while he was in the shower. We were "normal" people living our life.

My husband was the first person in my life to wholly trust in God for EVERYTHING. He went through the day constantly in prayer and praising Christ. He didn't worry. By watching him live his life, I learned by example that the answer to everything is in scripture and surrender to Him. All of this has come to me in the last 1,084 days.

When my husband was called Home I was devastated and, if I am honest, I was mad. I have never been so broken, spilled out and empty as I was after his death. I surrounded myself with friends who were prayer warriors. They prayed for me around the clock and pointed me to the Scripture. The more I looked to Scripture, the more I started to remember what I had seen every day of my relationship with my husband and the closer I drew to my Savior.

I have learned that there is nothing I have or will experience that the Savior has not experienced first-hand when He walked this earth. He experienced gut-wrenching sadness and wept over his friend's death (John 11:35). He felt loneliness (Mark 15:34). He asked the Father to be relieved from a trial, if possible (Mark 14:36). His friends who had promised loyalty weren't there every time He needed them (Mark 14:37).

I didn't learn this all at once. As I experienced each of these feelings and then turned to scripture, I had an awakening or a slow awareness that He knows the road I'm walking on. He knows the sorrow and emptiness I am feeling with the loss of my love. He knows the anger I feel at being separated from my husband. He knows the aching loneliness I feel. He knows I didn't want this, but He needed me to walk this journey and survive this trial. He knows how I feel when I call friends and they aren't available because they have had to continue their lives too. He knows all of this without me having to explain it.

He knows this because in His earthly body, He experienced all of this. But another reason He knows it, is because He has walked every step of my journey right beside me. He has never left my side. He has seen every tear, heard every sigh, listened to every word, and ached alongside me.

So, who better to talk to about this journey, than my Savior? Who better to share these feelings with? He understands and knows. I find comfort in this. I find comfort in the fact that the same Savior that loved my husband enough to free him from all the pain and suffering here and take him Home is looking after my every need.

1,085 days ago, I couldn't have imagined a moment without my husband and refused to let my mind go there. 1,084 days ago, I didn't think I would ever breathe again, much less live an abundant life. Now, here I am 1,084 days down this road and I can tell you that I still miss my husband very much, but my days are filled to overflowing with joy and Blessings. My days of laughter far outweigh my days of tears.

The secret is just taking one more step and surrendering each day to the One who made us and loves us and supplies our every need and drawing near to Him.

Draw near to God, and he will draw near to you.
James 4:8a ESV

September 28
Stepping Outside the Boat
By Nancy Howell

But Jesus spoke to them at once.
"Don't be afraid," he said. "Take courage. I am here!"
Then Peter called to him, "Lord, if it's really you, tell me to
come to you, walking on the water."
"Yes, come," Jesus said.
So Peter went over the side of the boat
and walked on the water toward Jesus.
But when he saw the strong wind and the waves,
he was terrified and began to sink.
"Save me, Lord!" he shouted.
Jesus immediately reached out and grabbed him.
"You have so little faith," Jesus said.
"Why did you doubt me?"
Matthew 14: 27-31 NLT

Fighting heavy waves...far from land...in the middle of the night...praying for relief....

Dear sisters, does this describe parts of your grief journey as you navigate the waters of life?

How many of you have cried out, frightened that the stormy waters and the waves will capsize the boat you are in?

In my marriage, I wasn't the captain of our ship. With a lot of patience and training, I became a pretty decent first mate, as my spouse and I sailed the sea of life. We had defined roles. I never steered, which was fine by me.

My husband was the consummate captain. He kept a close watch on the weather, he took all safety precautions, and made sure that we sailed on calm waters most every day of our life together.

Under his leadership, I never even thought about steering...I was content to be Gilligan to his Skipper, Mr. Spock to his Captain Kirk, jelly to his peanut butter. It's what worked for us, over the life of our marriage.

After losing him, I found myself lost. I'd never steered a boat. Overnight, it was dumped into my lap--all of it.

God, I don't know the first thing about navigating this boat. What am I supposed to do?

The ship is now in my hands, the first mate, the left-handed girl from Western Kentucky, who hasn't steered in twenty-three years. In the vessel with me are our two sons. They are certain I've got what it takes to lead them, even in the midst of the storm we've been pulled in to.

I cry out desperately, the sobs heaving in my chest, so loud that I can be heard over the high winds and crashing waves--I cry to my Father for help.

I see Jesus. He's walking on top of the storm,

the waves, the wake, the churning mess of life that's tossing my boat around. And with each step He takes, the waters lie calmly beneath.

He beckons me to come out of the vessel. This, dear sisters, is the ultimate stretch for me. I don't think "outside of the boat." I have a well-defined comfort zone, most happy while I am within its parameters, where I feel safe and secure.

He's asking me to step out in faith. On the water. Without a life jacket. And walk towards Him.

Do I have the faith of Peter? Not by a long shot.

But I am comforted by Peter's very human response in the above passage. He steps out, and is doing great, as long as he keeps his eyes focused on Jesus. The waves, the wind, and the foaming sea begin to distract him--he takes his eyes off of his Savior--it is in that moment he begins to sink and drown. He cries out.

Jesus grabs him by the arm, saving him. And He asks, " You have so little faith! Why did you doubt me?"

I've been steering our little boat for almost two years now. We've had our share of storms, of downbursts and clouds. Jesus is once again asking me to come away from the wheel, step out of my comfort zone, and trust Him. He wants me to climb over the side of this boat, and step out onto the deep treacherous water.

He's pretty persistent when He needs to be--- and pretty hard to ignore.

So I step out. Out in faith. Out of my comfort zone. For His glory and His glory alone. He tells me that together we will do wondrous things for His kingdom.

I just hope I am up for the challenge.

Heavenly Father, Give me the confidence, the strength, and the know-how to steer this ship of life through whatever conditions that might be encountered. Whenever You come to me, walking on water, beckoning me to step out in faith, give me the strength to take that first step, to swing my legs over the side, and step onto the water, whether it is choppy, cold, or calm and crystal-clear. You and You alone have the power to calm the seas surrounding me. Help me step outside my comfort zones for Your glory. Amen

September 29
I GET To!
By Liz Anne Wright

> *Taste and see that the Lord is good;*
> *blessed is the one who takes refuge in him.*
> *Psalm 34:8 NIV*

When I was growing up, one of my dad's favorite phrases to us was, "If life gives you lemons, make lemonade." It was almost a family mantra. I am often called a "Pollyanna" and an "eternal optimist" because of it.

When my husband died, I used this same philosophy to get through all I was experiencing in grief. I tried to make the best of each and every situation. I did not avoid the pain and troubles, but instead looked at my new life as a series of challenges that I could take on to make something new.

I had a real revelation at church the other day, showing me just how far I have come in my grief and rebuilding.

I don't have to live this life...I GET to live this life!

Yep. My "new life" is pretty fantastic!

- I have the extreme joy of purposeful work as I continue to homeschool my sons and raise them to manhood in the image of, and to the glory of, their Heavenly Father.
- I have boatloads of friends who occupy my time and my heart.
- I have a warm, safe home to live in, and while I am not rolling in "dough", I get by comfortably, by the grace of God

And...I have my involvement with *A Widow's Might/aNew Season.* As I was working to prepare for one of our retreats, I kept having my socks knocked off by the ways the Lord blessed the time we will have and the ministry we will be doing. He has taken care of EVERY detail – and given us blessings which really blow my mind! We are working SEAMLESSLY as a team!

Dear sisters, this journey is painful...more so than I thought anything could be. It is so difficult to be without the one I loved best next to the Lord. Beyond that, there are the mechanics of living this life as a single mom...and a single woman. There are days that get me down and I have a little pity party.

But...we make a *choice* as to how we live.

- I *choose* to take what this life has given me...and make it *more*!
- I *choose* to carry on the work Keith and I began in

our boys and see it through to lead them to an ever-closer walk with Christ.

- I *choose* to share my world with all those around me, to let them see that they, too, can be *more*.
- I *choose* to keep close to my Lord and Savior and work to develop that relationship, despite my life circumstances (maybe because of them).

This new walk takes boldness, dear sisters…and perseverance. But…God is there every step of the way, every moment of the day. And…it is worth it!

One of my favorite scriptures is, oddly enough, John 16:33 NIV

I have told you these things, so that in me you may have peace. In this world you will have trouble. But take heart! I have overcome the world.

Jesus tells us straight off that it will be hard. Thus, we have no reason to be surprised. But…He also tells us that He will overcome. Amen and hallelujah!

All He wants us to do is *keep trying*.

I know you are all in different places in your grief journey. I know you may not be at the "I GET to" stage yet. But, dear sisters, *persevere*. God's got this, and will reveal your new life to you in His time and for His glory.

While the lemonade may start out tangy, even sour, on your tongue, by the end of the drink, it will be sweet.

Taste and see!

Dear Father, thank You for all the joy of not walking this journey alone, of my pain not being wasted. Thank You that in

Your economy, every bit of me is being remade to serve You better. Please, Lord, help me taste You and see that You...and this new life...are good. In Jesus' Name, Amen.

September 30
Assembly Required
By Kit Hinkle

Jesus looked at them and said, "With man this is impossible, but with God all things are possible."
Matthew 19:26 NIV

"Mom, can you help me fly my airplane?" Carter asked this weekend on his eighth birthday.

Here was something that hadn't occurred to me. After the party guests go home, after the house is tidied up and we all take that breather from the pounding noise at the Chuck E Cheese-equivalent we just experienced, my son would want to share his sweet gifts with me.

I have a college education, and believe it or not, an engineering degree. But still I get a bit daunted by this type of request. "Remote control", "kit", "assembly required" - these were buzzwords that translated to *Dad's job*! After a while, it became convenient for me to rely on him for tackling these projects while I tended to our home.

Today I let the laundry sit. My son needed help with his airplane, so I sat with him at the table. He watched me with eyes that anticipated, "Mom knows what she's doing". Taking a deep breath to relax my butterflies, I carefully read the instructions with him and we assembled, charged the batteries, and took the plane for its virgin flight.

I had forgotten what a feeling of success these types of toys can bring. With every successful flight, I felt a zing of confidence building in me. If I can handle this, I might be able to handle the hovercraft he got, and then the trebuchet model kit the boys have waiting to be assembled. Perhaps I might even graduate to the Snap Circuits integrated circuit board kit (okay, even with an engineering degree- that might be pushing it!).

It occurred to me that what's really being assembled is my heart. It's not a sacrifice to handle Tom's traditional role of toy assembly parent; it's an honor. I now know why Tom gladly jumped at this job- it was one of his ways of teaching joy, his greatest legacy, to our boys.

Tom was so good at having fun that like many married couples, we tended to allow that fun role to go to him, while I carried on with some of the necessary household duties. Now the Lord is challenging me to find that right balance of tasks versus fun with the kids.

Lord, help me to continue to assemble the pieces of my heart. As strange as it sounds, I thank you for the situation I'm in. There is joy in the struggle, but knowing that without Your will allowing me to walk without my loved one, I may never allow myself to fully experience the joy another struggle brings. You've prepared me with everything I need to raise children in Your grace to become adults who will glorify You throughout their lives. Amen

October

October 1
Conquering the Pity Party
By Kit Hinkle

It is of the LORD's mercies that we are not consumed,
because his compassions fail not.
They are new every morning:
great is thy faithfulness.
Lamentations 3:22-23 KJV

Sometimes for me, even after years of going it alone, a bout of tears will hit. I think it hits everyone. Widowed or not, life can be tough. My typical weak-moment comes occasionally and unexpectedly. When it does, it's usually at about three in the afternoon when all points of stress converge on a single mother with four kids and no living parents to help raise them.

Let me describe it to you and see if you relate. Feel free to skip on down past this description because it's quite a pity party (smile)—one I don't like to share because I hate complaining.

Here it goes… I'm tired. All four kids pull me in four directions—someone needs to be picked up from school, another has a huge project due, and the younger two keep climbing that tree in the front yard that's not meant to hold their weight (as the neighbor has so "politely" told me)! The dog just swallowed another sock and the laundry needs folding before it wrinkles. The microwave's broken and the countertop has a crack in it.

If that isn't enough to tear my hair out, the longing for the life before widowhood creeps in. It hits in the form of rejection. It's in the air, something in the change of the weather that triggers some memories. Maybe it's the certain time of the year when one of those couple friends my hubby and I hung with has a party. We used to go every year to it. Without a husband, the invitations stopped coming. I glance at the calendar and my blood pressure goes up. Why can't they at least invite me? Let me decide if I don't want to be a fifth wheel?

I feel alone and abandoned. I start grasping to remember who's called recently. The phone only rang today with routine stuff—nothing social. But then I tell myself, who needs the social? There are kids to raise, work to do. I don't have time for social, and the last time I went to one of those gatherings where everyone had a husband but me the fellowship with others didn't satisfy me in the way I long for. It doesn't wake up every morning by my side and make life plans with me. Oh, how alone. My life is just work. Toil. Kids. Repairs. Why does everyone else get to have a companion? Why am I stuck being alone? The pain. The void. It's so ugly.

Okay, I'll stop. This is embarrassing!

Perhaps I'm hard on myself, but I think I sound ridiculous! I do go through those bouts of wallowing, but here's where I've changed. I've learned to recognize how ungodly and full of lies those thoughts are. And having already observed those thoughts as a habit, I can take a further step to eliminate them.

What I do is remember the last time I felt this way. I remember how it blew over and I looked back and realized what a lie it was. I know the truth. I'm not alone. Not abandoned. My friends and I connect a lot and like me, they have busy days. That couple didn't invite me because they didn't want me to be uncomfortable at a gathering of couples—it's not rejection. My life isn't just toil. It has huge significance and purpose and I laugh a lot. I do get breaks from the kids. And as far as a companion, if it's a longing in my heart, God will give me a companion. I'll trust.

So what to do with the pity party?

I stand on Truth.

I've learned to sing one of my favorite hymns and focus on the words "Morning by morning new mercies I see." Yes, it's "*Great is Thy Faithfulness*". Don't you just love that song? When Thomas Chisholm wrote the lyrics in the mid 1900's, he was inspired by Lamentations 3:22-23

"*It is of the LORD's mercies that we are not consumed, because his compassions fail not. They are new every morning: great is thy faithfulness.*"

When we are at our darkest hour, we remember that the sun will come up and His mercies are new and the Truth will obliterate the self-pitying lies we are so susceptible to.

God loves you. **He will bring you joy and love and companionship to fill your needs.** When you've had a good wallow and you get to that point when you are ready to get up from the tears, repeat that truth written in bold face above out loud. If it doesn't pull you out, repeat it again.

Then, begin to "Act as if". It's a great trick. Try it. It tricks Satan—foils his ploy. You look at the feelings you have and you simply state, "I've been here before, and these lies have been exposed before. These are only feelings, not truth. I know the Truth."

Then move forward. In spite of the pain. You "act as if" you weren't in pain even though you feel it. Push through it. Get up and get something done. Wash the dishes. Get those clothes put away. Play monopoly with the kids. God smiles on that. The enemy packs his bag and leaves your mind. You're better.

Father God, allow me to see Your mercies today. Your faithfulness is so great but sometimes I miss it by focusing on myself. I want to push through my pain today and see true healing that comes only from You. Amen

October 2
The Night My Life Changed...Forever
By Leah Stirewalt

*Though the fig tree does not bud and
there are no grapes on the vines,
though the olive crop fails and the
fields produce no food,
though there are no sheep in the pen
and no cattle in the stalls,
yet, I will rejoice in the Lord, I will be
joyful in God my Savior.*
Habakkuk 3:17-18 NIV

He never missed an episode of *The Biggest
Loser*. As unpredictable as we might be at other times,
one certainty remained…our family would spend
most Tuesday evenings in front of the TV watching
NBC's ever popular *The Biggest Loser*. So, when my
husband wasn't home by *Loser's* start time of eight
p.m., I knew something must be wrong.

After getting off work, I called my husband,
as I practiced daily, to tell him I was on my way
home. He never answered, but I left a voicemail,
followed by a text. Upon receiving no replies from my
texts, phone calls, or voice mails, I grew very
concerned.

So many of the details are still fuzzy, but
several hours later, I vividly remember sitting in the
police station with my friend and my teenage
daughter thinking, "When will this nightmare end?
This can't be happening." I answered question after
question from the officer. Of course, they assumed
Chris just needed a night away and would turn back
up tomorrow. Seriously? Without telling me first? I
realized they probably dealt with cases like this every
single day. But, I had to get them to understand…my

husband was different.

My husband and I were madly in love. He treated me like a princess. We lived like newlyweds virtually every single day. Our honeymoon never ended. I was his queen, and he was my king. He would never do anything to intentionally harm me. Never. Therefore, I knew something must be wrong.

After several hours in the police station filing my "missing husband" report, I went home. A pastor friend later arrived, and we set out around two a.m. to search for Chris' red truck, since the police were of no help at this point. The fog was so thick that night we could barely see our hand in front of us. We never discovered his truck.

Fast forwarding through this blur of nearly twenty-four hours, my Connect Group from church formed a search team. The police were able to narrow down the area to a twelve-mile radius, thanks to cell phone pings. But even this radius seemed daunting due to the terrain (mostly dense forest).

That afternoon, I received the call I had been praying for. One of the men from my Connect Group uttered the words I'll never forget, "Leah, we've found the truck. Chris isn't in it, but we're looking for him now." I started sobbing out of relief. The truck had been found. At least that was SOMETHING! But, the sobbing turned to fear, because I knew something had to be wrong. A few hours later I had my answer.

The group walked into my home. This group of my closest church friends who had been involved in the search, led by the pastor friend who had been out in the middle of the night with me searching for Chris in the fog. As soon as I saw their faces, I knew the outcome. I just didn't know the specifics.

I walked into my bedroom and was followed by several friends. I wanted to get as far away from the crowd as I could for fear of the words I was about to hear. As the words came, my heart collapsed, followed by my body.

I was told Chris was found, but not alive. Even more shocking, I was told that my precious husband had taken his own life. "Impossible. There's no way my husband would do this. He was one of the happiest people I knew," my thoughts said. And, yet, he did. The proof came later...my husband did, in fact, take his own life.

In spite of the pain of that first night and the following day, I share this with absolute confidence that...

My God is still in control.

He is still abundantly good.

Without Him, I am nothing.

But, with Him...I can do all things.

With Him, I can do "hard".

A few years later, I am soaking in life again, living proof of His ongoing restoration work.

I know that Chris loved the Lord with all his heart! He had been a believer for many, many years. He was just very sick at the end of his life and not in his right mind. The Lord was with him that night, as He was welcomed into Heaven. The same night, the Lord was with me and caught every single tear I shed.

Father God, thank You for catching every single tear I shed. You know my difficult story. You know my difficult situation. You know. Yet, I will rejoice in You. Yet, I will praise You. Amen

October 3
Steadfast
By Linda Lint

The steadfast love of the Lord never ceases.
Lamentations 3:22 ESV

Shortly after we moved to this area I became fascinated with windmill lawn ornaments. It seemed they were everywhere in various sizes and colors. People painted them to match their houses or in their favorite team colors--I wanted one. However, our budget was tight and it was one of those "wants" that slipped down on the list. Then one spring day we saw the ad at the same time. They were on sale - at an affordable price! My beloved said, "Let's go get one".

The box said *assembly required.* Now that was an understatement! Not only did our windmill consist of many larger metal pieces, but the box held a huge number of incredibly tiny screws, nuts and bolts. The assembly took my husband practically all day. His hands were so large, yet the screws so tiny. He would periodically pause and rest, because his hands would ache. After the assembly was complete, he had to anchor it in the ground and level it. It was, indeed, a full day's work. He did it all because of the love he had for me.

That was over fifteen years ago. That windmill has remained - standing firm against torrential rains, fierce winds, pelting hail and winter's cold. It has been a resting point for birds as they come to eat the seeds of the flowers that grow beneath it. And it is a daily reminder of my husband's love for me, for it is the first thing I see when I raise the shade on the kitchen window.

It is a gift he did not have to give. That's what makes it so very special.

There is another gift I have been given. It, too, is a gift of immeasurable love.

It is also represented by a structure - that of a wooden cross.

My windmill is a reminder of the earthly love of my husband. The cross is the assurance of God's eternal love for me.

God's love is steadfast and never ceasing. It is a love that has stood guard over me through grief's storms, and given me a place to rest.

That windmill will not last forever. Eventually it will deteriorate with age.

The love that the Father has for me - and for you, dear reader - has stood the test of time, and will last forever.

As I approach the two year mark of my beloved's passing, I humbly give thanks to a God who loves me beyond measure - He gave His only Son so I could spend eternity with Him. I thank Him for the twenty-five years my husband and I had together, the love we shared, the windmill, and most importantly - I thank Him for the cross.

Dear Father, give me the knowledge of Your steadfast love. Touch my hurting heart, giving me peace. Amen

October 4
Walking the Tight-Rope
By Elizabeth Dyer

She is clothed with strength and dignity;
she can laugh at the days to come.

Proverbs 31:25 NIV

I didn't watch the live coverage of the tight-rope walker on TV, since I rarely even turn the TV on any more since my husband passed away. It could also have been because I seem to be walking my OWN tight-rope, though mine is not nearly so high but ever-so-emotionally death-defying. And trying to do it with "strength and dignity" is more difficult than just laughing at the future. I do well at finding the humor in situations. I just lack the dignity!

The tight-rope I am walking is between overwhelmed and over-confident. I can swing between the two hourly, daily.

I returned home from our first family trip post-daddy with great confidence. I had done the long driving by myself. I had ridden roller coasters. I had been Mom-of-the-year. I got the single parenting thing down. Watch me go!

And then it happened. Reality struck after getting back into the swing of things. Several events shook me up. And every situation was a picture of how my husband and I dealt with the issues differently. Over-confidence at thinking I got it figured out, and overwhelmed when I find out I don't. Where is the strength and dignity?

One situation was with the mower. We live on nearly an acre, so cutting the grass takes a while. After charging the mower's battery, as was the norm with this irritating mower, I had finally hit an all-time low. *(Insert sarcastic voice here)* And knowing that being bitter and angry makes the kind act you are doing so much better, I growled and complained the whole way around the yard as I did the mowing. Nice example of "strength and dignity" if there ever was one!

Picture this: family sitting around table enjoying corn dogs mom had put in the oven to cook while mom, in her (modest) swim suit, was out mowing the yard. I came in and went "psycho-mom" on them. I wondered aloud how much grass would I have to cut before any of them felt any guilt?

One said, "I thought you wanted to cut the grass."

Really, son? What I said was, "I want the grass cut." A large canyon separates those two statements!

The other problem was that there is something wrong with the mower since it has to be jump-started at each use. My husband was the charging master, having been doing it to his cars since time began. He kept the mower battery charged and starting.

The last straw was the tile removal in the master bath. I have never really assisted in any remodeling projects because we just talked about change but never really did it. So when several church men said they would help me re-tile my bathroom, I took them up on it. My boys could get the job started, they said. No problem, I thought. How hard can it be?

I turned two teens lose with a mallet, sledge hammer, hammer, and a crow bar. My husband would have taken forty-five minutes to show them how to do it, demonstrate, talk about it until they were bored to tears, then help them prep the room.

So I am balancing between thinking I can and knowing I can't. I bought a new mower, giving the old one to a friend, who may never speak to me again. One of my teens loved the new mower so much he slalomed around the trees, having fun! Small price to pay for getting a fifteen year old to ask to cut the grass! I guess getting his favorite color will work to my advantage!

I really do want to be a better example of "strength and "dignity", especially to my girls. They need to see that my strength and dignity come from somewhere outside myself, from God and the time I spend with Him in Scripture.

How are you doing balancing your tight-rope?

Your tight-rope might be between grief and joy, worldly advice and Scripture teaching, or wanting to be loved again and not wanting to replace your first love. Whatever your tight-rope is, walk it with a strength and dignity that others will notice is from ABOVE and not from what the world offers.

Heavenly Father, thank You that You created me and You have plans for my life. Give me the desire to spend time in Scripture to regain my focus for the day. I pray for strength and dignity today as I walk the tight-rope in my life. And help me to see the humor in some of life's situations. Amen

October 5
Paddling Through the Eighteenth Month
By Karen Emberlin

The Lord will be your everlasting light,
and your days of sorrow will end
Isaiah 60:20 NIV

Grief - it has been said by many that there is no right or wrong way to grieve, and it is not a sign of weakness or lack of faith – *Grief is the price we pay for love.*

I was introduced to this thing called "grief" when my husband suddenly made his journey to heaven.

Grief became my constant companion. Many changes took place. First, there was shock that left me numb, empty and in a fog, making it difficult to function. Then came physical changes (weight loss and sleepless nights), emotional changes (anxious thoughts about my future), lifestyle changes (a move to another state), social changes (wondering who I actually am), and spiritual change (trying to decide God's will for me). With time, some of the initial feelings of grief have lightened as decisions have been made and details were worked out. But heartache and loneliness continue, as the realization of the loss of my husband deepens. Realizing the finality of death leaves such a hollow empty feeling over my whole being.

Eighteen months have passed, and most people think I'm supposed to be "getting over my loss" and "getting back to normal". People look at me on the "outside" and think it's true. Ducks are such perfect examples. Sometimes I feel like the duck that looks calm on the outside but is paddling as hard as it can to stay afloat!

I have made progress, but those looking on the "outside" do not see the pain still weighing down on the "inside". Most people resume their busy schedules, and as long as I do not appear to be broken, they think I'm okay.

While those around me respond to what they see from the "outside", God sees me from the "inside"! He is aware of my circumstances, my pain, and my emptiness. The death of my husband was no surprise to Him. He knew I would be a widow – He also knows this is not the end of my life!

Please understand, I will be the first to tell you how blessed I am and how much I do not like feeling so "unsettled" inside. Even when grief causes me to feel alone, afraid, and sorry for myself I still have the assurance that He will never leave me or forsake me! Because He is Lord over every loss and heartache, He also is the Lord of all comfort and compassion. I may not know how long this process will take, but He promises that my days of sorrow will end!

Lord, I know that You care for me and understand the struggles and feelings I experience. Fill me with hope and help me look forward to the day You complete the work You began in me. Help me grow in You and live with a passion and purpose for You. Open doors that will allow me to share the love You have for me and encourage others that "weeping may endure for a night, but joy cometh in the morning". Amen

October 6
Are You Feeling Weak?
By Sheryl Pepple

That is why, for Christ's sake, I delight in weaknesses,
in insults, in hardships, in persecutions, in difficulties.
For when I am weak, then I am strong.
2 Corinthians 12:10 NIV

Have you seen it yet, my dear sister? God's glory being shown through you when you are weak, just as the Apostle Paul described in Corinthians? If you have not yet seen it or had someone share it with you how they see it, then please pray and ask Him to reveal it to you. It is such a blessing to know that He is bringing good out of one of the most difficult times in our lives.

The first time God made me aware of this truth about strength in my life was during my brother's funeral when I was twenty-nine years old. My sweet brother was murdered on his twenty-fourth birthday while riding his bike to work. It was a random act of violence; they think that he rode up during a drug deal and he was shot to death. It made front page news for many days while they tried to solve the crime.

As a result, my brother's funeral was attended by hundreds of strangers and the media was there in full force. In the midst of walking around in a state of shock at the funeral, one of the reporters from a major newspaper cornered me for a comment. Out of my mouth came the quote "I think it is so special that God called my brother home for his birthday." It turned out that moment was a gift from God that had a profound impact in my Christian walk. He used it as an important spiritual marker in my life, to show me that in my weakest moment His strength was manifested in me, and bringing good out of a terribly difficult time.

Fast forward several years and I am once again thrust into the murder of a family member, but this time it was my precious husband driving to work, killed by a drunk driver. (It is classified as a murder because of the responsible party's previous DUI convictions.) I am once again thrust into a state of shock and grief. And even in the midst of the shock and pain, God reminded me once again that when I am weak, then I am strong.

Sometimes, God shows me how His strength is magnified through me during this journey. I remember the day one of my friends shared with me that she now knew that no matter what she faced in life, she knew that her faith would sustain her, because she had seen how God did that for me. What a precious gift!

Another way God blessed me by demonstrating His strength through me was during several testimonies I had to give in various courts (worker's compensation case and criminal case). Each time it was overwhelmingly apparent it was God who made me strong when I was weak and that He was the one who enabled me to do what had to be done.

My daughters were there to support me and I know God added to their faith by showing His strength through me during those situations. They knew it was not my strength. I was weak, and then by His power I was strong.

And yet, sometimes in this journey I still forget that God will give me the strength that will carry me through. I have worried about so many things, but one of my biggest worries has been doing my job adequately. I had so much going on with various court cases, and, as you know, the grief is so overwhelming. I can't tell you how much I agonized about my job. I am very blessed that I get to do something I love - I get to help people get into Biblical community as the director of Small Groups at my church.

One day when I was pouring out all of my concerns and worries to one of my mentors, about being able to do my job, she stopped me and said, "Don't you realize, God is teaching our church more about Biblical community through you in a way you never could?" Wow, my weakness turned into strength by God in yet another way.

In many ways our journeys are the same, and yet the circumstances are often very different. But for each of us, God is faithful. He will be true to His nature, He cannot lie. Like Paul, we can delight in knowing that in our weakness He will be there, He will carry us through, our faith will grow. For when we are weak, then we are strong!

Dear Heavenly Father, I praise You for Who You are. You are the maker of the heavens and the earth. You are my Redeemer and Savior. Thank You for providing for my every need for being my strength during this journey. I thank You, Father, for all You are doing through me during this season for Your kingdom, for Your glory. Help me keep my eyes focused on You and to walk in obedience. Your grace is sufficient for me. Father, please strengthen and encourage me today, and continue to reveal how our weaknesses are being turned into strength, for Your glory! In Jesus's name. Amen.

October 7
What's Your Question?
By Teri Cox

*Create in me a clean heart, O God.
Renew a loyal spirit within me.
Do not banish me from your presence,
and don't take your Holy Spirit from me.
Restore to me the joy of your salvation,
and make me willing to obey you.*
Psalm 51:10-12 NLT

I must admit that after my husband died, my husband of twelve years, I struggled at times with "joy" and feeling God's presence. I KNEW that God had not abandoned me, but the blanket of grief I wore caused me to feel less than treasured, less than chosen, less than loved by my Heavenly Father.

Many days, I simply felt less than; less than myself, less than people around me, less than I had been, less than I wanted to be. I was missing half of myself and by my own admission, he was the better half. He was the one who was patient, and kind, quick to listen and slow to anger; he was the one who grounded me with his rock steady way of living life, loving people, and being an example of Christ and servanthood. He was older and wiser. He was a picture of stability and I, well I, was a mess.

Sometimes, I even found it hard to pray. I had SO MANY questions that seemed to have no answers. What was God's purpose in all of this? Why? I knew that the Holy Spirit would cry out for me when I could not do it for myself:

Romans 8:26, Likewise the Spirit helps us in our weakness. For we do not know what to pray for as we ought, but the Spirit himself intercedes for us with groanings too deep for words. ESV

Some days all I could pray was, "Jesus", but slowly I began to pray for "joy"-**the joy of the Lord**. Not the happiness of the world that centers around things, but "joy" that comes from being so interwoven with God's Spirit that you can hear His whisper in your ear. The kind of "joy" that leaves you speechless and in awe of a Father who adores His precious children; that's the "joy" I prayed for and my perspective began to change.

I had to move past the question, "Why" to "Now What." I learned that "Why" requires a response from God that I may never get, but "Now What", that requires a response from me. I don't have to like it but I do have to MOVE and be obedient to what God asks me to do. So, "Now What" has become my question. I have been surprised at how the change of question has brought me to obedience and fullness of "joy". **My perspective changed because my question changed.**

Lord, Help me cling to You more than ever before and to lean in and lean on Your Word. Give me the right question to help me move forward down the path You have chosen for me, trusting You are with me. Help me to focus me eyes on You. Amen.

October 8
A New Signature
By Kit Hinkle

> *Before I formed you in the womb I knew you,*
> *before you were born I set you apart;*
> *I appointed you as a prophet to the nations.*
> *Jeremiah 1:5 NIV*

It occurred to me.

Looking at the calendar, I realized that my time in this home has been spent more as a single mom than married.

How could that be when it seems only yesterday he was here? My memories of life with Tom and the four boys seem to fill most of that space in my heart called "living in North Carolina".

In that first year I never needed to tell anyone. It was out there, because everyone was shocked. Tom was too young for heart attacks. My entire community came out to love on the boys and me.

It was at the two-year mark when it dawned on me it's not the newest news anymore. While getting ready to speak at my church, I mentioned backstage that many there already know what happened with my husband. The pastor gently interrupted. "Actually, Kit, there are so many new people in this church now. I bet most don't even know you're widowed."

As years pass, I'm faced with more and more new people in my life so I have to decide whether to explain. Early on I almost felt like it was my right to tell people. I missed Tom and I wanted everyone to remember him, never forget that only half of me was here.

But I started to reclaim my other half. I've found more meaningful ways to memorialize him without having to carry a "sign" on me saying, "Remember Tom!" I write about him, and share stories and photos with family. Last fall I put together a huge photo book for my older stepchildren, full of photos of him from as far back as their birth.

Another reason I would mention to people I'm widowed is perhaps I felt guilty for surviving him and moving forward without him. Time heals that wound, and the guilt passes with the grace of God.

Time alone does miracles on your soul. God has a way of using it to carve out every bit of pride, and I'm now finding that worrying over how people view my status as a single mom is all pride.

I've let that go. God knows what a great husband he was. I don't need to hold up a banner.

So now I just let people learn about Tom as the subject arises. Once the loss is no longer fresh, volunteering the fact that my husband died can invite sympathy at moments when I'm really not looking for it. I'm glad people are compassionate, and I love when they share stories of God's grace in difficult situations. But **I use His Grace, not my loss, as a signature.** I'd rather others notice how God completes me by helping me manage my household and future wisely. I'd rather they see my faith and be surprised at what I'd been through. That surprise is **my signature of God's Grace**.

Recently I hosted a meeting of homeschooled families in my home. Several of the moms were new acquaintances, and I suppose it's unusual to have a widowed mother continue her homeschooling alone. So naturally, they assumed I was married.

On two separate occasions someone mentioned husbands.

"Does your husband take the boys out fishing?" one asked.

"Let's get the husbands involved in this homeschool project," another said.

What a dilemma that used to create for me. Now I relax and let God speak through me. I sweetly let each know with no hesitation or embarrassment, "Oh, I wish I could include Tom. You probably don't know yet, but we lost him a few years ago."

I've found there's no easy way to say it without the other person responding, "Oh!" and turning the conversation into a grief support moment.

I've learned how to diffuse that right away, by reassuring them that this isn't a fresh or open wound and it's totally okay for them to speak of my husband and my situation.

One of the two women who raised the subject of husbands responded with admiration to me, telling me I'm doing great, to which I answered it isn't me. "This is all God's doing," I stated. She didn't hesitate and her conversation moved forward without a hitch. This is a testimony to God's grace in restoring me to function and socialize over three years out, without the loss of my husband being a conversation stopper.

It's all part of the signature God wants us to have. Not Kit the Widow, and Not Kit the Survivor, but **Kit, a testimony to God's Grace and Power**.

I pray that the Lord moves in you and turns your signature and the way people are impacted by you into a testimony for Him.

October 9
Run This Race
By Erika Graham

For the moment
all discipline seems painful rather than pleasant,
but later it yields the peaceful fruit of righteousness
to those who have been trained by it.
Therefore lift your drooping hands and
strengthen your weak knees, and make straight paths.
Hebrews 12:11-13 ESV

I run! If my husband were here he'd say something snarky like, "Yes, to a good sale at the store." See, the girl he knew didn't run. She loved and played sports of every kind, but running, to her, was just a way to conjure up bad memories. I played basketball throughout my life, all the way to the collegiate level. In my sport, running was the punishment.

Now, I'm not a runner, but I do run. I decided to start running a few months after my husband's passing. I thought it might be a good new thing and would help relieve stress. Mostly, I believed

I could honor my runner-hubby every time I hit the pavement because he was an avid runner whose crowning glory was running the NYC Marathon. I started small, and it was tough. I would still say, over three years later, when I run, I'm in a battle, my heart versus my mind and body. My heart wants to do this, but the body wants to quit with each step. When a friend saw me running one time, she thought I looked intense. I explained that I'm talking myself down from stopping the entire time.

I'm not a runner, but I do run. I completed my first 5k, one right in my hometown, a few months after starting. I gained confidence and began to participate in other area 5ks. I also found the fun world of mud runs. (If you've never tried one, I highly recommend it.) It's a fun crazy muddy run, with obstacles of all kinds thrown in. On the second anniversary of my husband's passing, I did a five mile mud run.

Did I mention I am not a runner, but I do run?

I was really getting ambitious (or crazy), so I signed up to run a half marathon, 13.1 whopping miles. I enlisted help from a dear friend, and we trained and ran the race together. Without our partnership, I don't think either of us would have finished the race because it was so gruelling. We were able to help each other, encourage each other, challenge each other, and, at certain points during the race, literally drag each other. She was an inspiration to me and was there to lovingly hold me accountable, support me, and be there by my side the whole time.

I realize now God is using running and particularly the half marathon to speak to me. He even used that race and the partnership with my dear friend to remind me of how much I need Him on this widow journey. He is there for me each step of the way, to love on me, support me, guide me, and literally push me forward or even carry me at times.

This widow "race" can be gruelling and overwhelming, and I could be easily disjointed or injured by my hurt and pain. But, like the verse from Hebrews assures me, God will bring "peaceful fruit" of righteousness out of my suffering, and He will protect the "lame parts" in my widowed heart. I am called to lift up my hands, strengthen my knees (I envision standing before Him with locked knees and open hands) and look to Him. He will heal me!

Heavenly Father, help me see Your working in my life. Help me be assured that my painful journey will yield fruit. Lord, bring me peace in my training, knowing that You are going to heal me and help ne move forward in Your perfect time. Protect my lame parts and guide me to straight healing paths in You. Lord, give me the strength and provision to run this race. In your matchless Name, Amen.

October 10
The Last Gift
By Liz Anne Wright

*And let us consider how we may spur one another
on toward love and good deeds,
not giving up meeting together,
as some are in the habit of doing,
but encouraging one another—
and all the more as you see the Day approaching.*
Hebrews 10:24-25 NIV

I celebrated my eighteenth wedding anniversary…alone. Two days before that, I celebrated the sixth anniversary of my sweet husband's arrival in Heaven…and mourned again my loss of him.

Sisters, the road is not the same each year as you continue to travel. Anniversaries, birthdays, and special days still hit me, but the magnitude is different, and I tend to remember more of the sweet memories than the pain.

This year, I am remembering a sweet, sweet story about my husband and my friends that shows just how blessed I am

As our anniversary approached six years ago, Keith and I decided not to get each other gifts. We would wait and go away for a weekend after he got better. He had been sick for several months with protein adhered to his heart, and was due for a heart biopsy the week after our anniversary.

That, however, was not meant to be.

Two days before our anniversary, he collapsed, was taken to the hospital, and passed away within the hour. With the support of family and friends, I began this widow walk.

When I returned home, I found the perfect parting gift from my sweet husband. Unbeknownst to me, he had ordered a dozen roses for our anniversary. They were beautiful. And I cried.

The day after receiving this gift, I did what some would not consider doing...I sent those flowers away.

It was not because they were hurtful. In fact, they were just the opposite. They brought me joy and comfort at a horribly difficult time.

And the sweet ladies at my church knew that.

The story of the flowers circulated almost as quickly as the calls regarding Keith's death. I think there were more tears cried by others in our church than by me that day, over Keith's sweet, last gift. Because they were so touched, these dear ladies spent much time and effort the day of Keith's death finding a person who could preserve those flowers for me.

The day after Keith died, they shipped my lovely flowers to a woman who freeze-dried them for preservation. They now hang in my bedroom as a beautiful reminder of how much Keith loved me.

And as a reminder of how much my friends loved me.

That day I began the same journey that you also walk. Your circumstances may be different, but the loss, the devastation, is the same.

By letting go of my flowers that first day, when I wanted so much to hold them to my face and weep into them, I gave way for God to work in incredible ways.

Other people were touched by the saga of the flowers as they journeyed away from me and back again, preserved. The young woman at the packaging store, who had not yet given her life to the Lord, heard the story and cried. My own congregation had a deepened sense of love and commitment to each other simply because I continued to share my life with them, even through these hard times.

As the boys and I share this journey with our church friends and family, there continues to be a deep and abiding bond that grows with each passing year.

It is not always easy to let others in, to admit that I cannot do things on my own, but the rewards to *all* are worth my discomfort. We are blessed tremendously…and, in turn, others are blessed by blessing us.

We were intended to walk this earth and live this life in <u>community</u>. That did not change with the loss of our spouses.

Let them in, sweet sisters, let them in. You need them and they need you. And by you letting them in, God will be glorified.

Dear Father, it is often so hard to walk this widow walk, to live with all the uncertainty and need! But I know that You created me in community for a purpose, Lord. Help me to see my purpose in my church and in my world. Help me be satisfied if that purpose is to be a receiver now, and not so much a giver. Help me realize that inviting people into my life is a gift I can give them. Help me to break down the walls of my pride and pain and allow others in. In the precious Name of Jesus I pray, Amen.

October 11

Empty Corner
By Linda Lint

If God is for us, who can be against us?
Romans 8:31 NIV

He was so special – that man I loved. It seemed that in his eyes I could do nothing wrong. Even when the broccoli was "overdone", he sprinkled it with some salt, added some butter and convinced the girls that this was a "special" recipe. And when the biscuits were a little too brown on the bottom he patiently took a sharp knife and shaved off the offending parts.

At times when I said, "I don't think I can do that," he said "Yes, you can. You're my wife."

He was ever-present, with a strong shoulder to lean upon and fortifying words of encouragement. Even in the care center in the last weeks of his life, when a staff member was less than pleasant with me, he quickly took her to task. He was always on my side.

He was in my corner.

And, having that assurance, I was able to move confidently through the days of motherhood at forty-two, rebellious teenagers, my job with special needs students, adjusting to winters in the Midwest, and so much more.

As I wandered through those early months of widowhood, the emptiness of that corner was so very painful. Making decisions was daunting. Learning something new was unthinkable. I longed to hear an "'atta girl" or "you're doing well". Yes, my children and friends were present with their encouragement and love – but it wasn't the same. Nothing could replace the words I heard from him.

Then I came upon Romans 8:31 in the Message Bible: *With God on our side, how can we lose?* Making it more personal, I rephrased it, *"Linda, with God on your side, how can you lose?"*

God is on my side! (And yours too!)

He defends the cause of the widow Deuteronomy 10:18 NIV

The Lord sets the widow's boundary stones in place Proverbs 15:25 NIV

I will contend with those who contend with you Isaiah 49:25 NIV

God has always been on my side; ever-present with a strong shoulder, sending messages of encouragement throughout the scriptures, defending me against all the "enemies" of loneliness and uncertainty.

God is in my corner.

Now, as I quietly move into the fourth year of widowhood, I will remember what He promised in *Jeremiah 29:13, When you come looking for Me, you will find Me.*(I'll be in your corner)

Dear Father, learning to live without the encouragement of my husband is so very difficult. I ask You, please, gently lead me to a place of understanding how much You love. Teach me how to listen for Your voice in the quiet, encouraging me and letting me know You are always on my side and in my corner. Amen

October 12
Discovering Me
By Rene Zonner

The thief comes only to steal and kill and destroy;
I have come that they may have life, and have it to the full.
John 10:10 NIV

Who am I now?

What do I want my life to look like?

How do I even start to figure it out?

These were all questions I found myself asking once I had worked through the earliest days of my grief.

For each of us it's different, but I believe we all will come to a point on this journey where we have "done the work" of getting through the grief. Oh, I'm not saying the grief is gone... I don't know that it ever goes away completely. I'm talking about that time when you wake up one morning and realize you are starting to look forward to the future. When you have truly accepted that it's okay for life to go on.

It's a good feeling, until reality hits.

I had been married for almost fourteen years, had dated my husband for two years before we got married. For sixteen out of my forty years on this earth, my life was linked to his. I cooked food that catered to both our tastes, I watched TV shows that he liked because I didn't have much of a preference. We went to movies that would appeal to both of us. He was a bit of a homebody so we didn't go out much. He was a stronger personality and had stronger likes and dislikes, so I found myself letting his preferences dictate our life together. That's not a bad thing, it's often part of being married.

But I'm not married anymore. So now what?

I knew I didn't want to keep doing things the way I had when my husband was alive. I wanted my life to look different but I had no idea what that meant for me and my kids. I began a journey of self-discovery during the years that have followed. I just began trying things. I declared one year to be The Year of Saying Yes. I had been widowed about a year and half at that point. I joined the singles group at my church and met new friends who opened me up to new experiences. I decided I would say yes whenever someone asked me to do something new.

I went dancing for the first time since college. Another single mom and I took our kids camping …in tents and cooked over the fire! The kids and I checked out some local festivals we'd never been to before. I went ice skating, hiking and jet skiing. I took the kids to the beach for the first time. I went back to attending the theater. I embraced the creative talent given to me by God and rediscovered my love for creating art. I got involved in ministry leadership. My kids and I started serving as a family in new ways at church.

I learned a lot about myself that year and I continue to discover more about who I am every day since. I have learned what kind of life I want to have as I move forward. God is using this time to reveal glimpses of how He plans to use me, where He wants me to go and what He wants my life to look like. God doesn't want us stuck. He wants us to have life and have it to the full, but we have to take the first steps to start discovering what that means.

So, who is Rene?

I am an artist, I am physically active, and I am not a homebody.

I love the beach, dancing and going to the theater.

I am a strong leader, I have ministry strengths that God is using in new ways, and I have an influence on lives I never realized before.

Who are you?

Our Dear Heavenly Father, I often feel unsure of who I am and what You want for my life. I pray for courage to step out of my comfort zone and try new things. I ask for guidance and direction about what the next step should be. I praise You for the amazing things You are going to do in my life. Thank You, Jesus, that You came to give me a full, abundant life and help me embrace this precious gift. Amen

October 13
Take Your Mark!
By Sherry Rickard

I do all this for the sake of the gospel,
that I may share in its blessings.
Do you not know that in a race all the runners run,
but only one gets the prize?
Run in such a way as to get the prize.
Everyone who competes in the games goes into strict training.
They do it to get a crown that will not last,
but we do it to get a crown that will last forever.
1 Corinthians 9:23-25 NIV

Have you ever seen a swim meet?

At the start of the race, the swimmer steps onto the starting block and bends over in the starting position. You can almost feel the muscles, full of energy poised, ready to race. The silence of the crowd, as they hold their breath and wait for the starting signal to sound, is palpable.

Have you ever seen a false start? Everyone in the entire pool area is waiting for the start signal and one (or more, sometimes) takes off before the signal. The release of breath from those present is almost like a gasp. The swimmer takes off down the length of the pool only to realize the race has not started.

They gave their all and it wasn't time to race…yet. They have to make their way back and climb out of the pool, shake off the excess water, get their head in the right place, and take their mark again. The entire energy of the area is changed as the swimmers again take their mark.

Think about the training involved for the swimmer to get to the point of being ready for the race. They have to do hours of repetitive strokes, perfecting their timing, the angle of their arms as they slice through the water, their turn at each end of the pool lane. It takes a coach who sees the end potential to push the swimmer beyond what they think they can do. It also involves conditioning. Swimmers have to run and lift weights too. They have to eat right and sleep right and have their thoughts on the end goal - competing and winning their race.

So, back to the swim meet. The swimmer has put the work in. The coach has put the work in. The swimmer puts his earphones in his ears to hear the song that gets him in "the zone" and waits for his heat to be called. Now, they get to the competition and they are ready to go and the crowd kicks in. The family is there screaming encouragement. He is ready!

I think this grieving journey is like that. We are called to walk this path - it's our pool. We have many false starts and have to get back to our starting place and try again. God puts "coaches" along the way to teach us; work with us; beckon to us to keep on "swimming"; people who sense God's calling in our life. We are asked to lift heavy things that, in the long run, grow us and make us stronger to handle heavier things further in our race. We listen to music that inspires us and read Scriptures that feed us. We have a Heavenly Father that gives us proper rest.

Then, as we prepare to swim our race, we hear our friends and family screaming encouragement from all around the pool area; whether it is a heartfelt prayer on our behalf, an encouraging phone call or an invitation to dinner. Their enthusiasm that we can win this race keeps us going. When we have the false starts, it is what gets us back to the poolside and back on the starting block.

God has specifically and lovingly chosen us for this race. He doesn't want us to experience grief, but He knows that we will be able to help others if we have walked a similar path and He can use our hands and feet to comfort others. He won't leave us and He will prepare us along the way.

Dear Lord, thank You for choosing me to glorify You. I don't see the strength that You see in me. I submit to Your Will, my loving Father. I know You will give me what I need and You will be with me as I run the race that You have set before me. I love you, Father, and with Your help I will finish this race. Amen

October 14
The Old Tin Ladle
By Jill Byard

I think of the old tin ladle I got to use while camping as a little girl on the northern shore of Lake Michigan.

I would make my way down from the very highest sand dune near Sturgeon Bay where the heat of the day made the black sand burn the soles of my feet. All I could think of was getting a taste of the best water ever to cool down.

Every time I dipped the ladle into the tin bucket of the fresh cold well water, the brisk Northern Michigan well water made the ladle handle cold to the touch, reassuring me that the drink that would follow would always satisfy my hot summer thirst--the kind of thirst you get from a long day of climbing the hot sand dunes and baking in the summer sun.

I think of our team of writers like that cold ladle. We are always reaching into fill ourselves with the only source that quenches. We are constantly going to the source and HE in turn fills us.

It says in *Isaiah 55:1, "Come, everyone who thirsts, come to the waters..."* So as our team brings our ladles to the waters of the river of Life, He fills them up and asks us to go and pour it out to our readers.

Just as the old tin ladle was a powerful tool

for quenching my thirst, this ministry is a powerful tool for quenching a thirst within our community. As our team of writers becomes filled, each of our ladles together makes a reservoir. We take our filled ladles and pour them out like waterfalls into our little rivers of social media, helping our readers find an oasis on their journey as they face struggles which leave them weary and thirsty.

Our individual ladles are tools being used to give our readers just a taste of the only source that will satisfy; our Jesus.

aNew Seasons Ministry has been an oasis for me as I connect with fellow sojourners on this journey. It's a place to be cooled by the shade and to drink in the reminders that even though we all may feel completely alone; we absolutely are not alone. As we walk hand in hand in unity on this path of sisterhood our voice can make an impact for the Kingdom.

So, dear sweet readers, when you do not feel like you are moving as fast as you want to or you just can't see beyond the ash heap, just know that if you keep moving it doesn't matter the pace, the key is to not stop for too long. He is preparing you for the top of the ash heap with every crawl and every tiny step.

He has you.

He goes before you, beside you, behind you and in front of you. He is making a way. He is getting ready to bring you to anew season and a place where He can shine through the cracks in your broken heart.

Now that I've poured from His oasis into your ladle-- whose ladle will you now fill with living water?

Dear Father, I love You and I am forever grateful for Your love for me. I want to trust You and live to bring You honor in all I do. I praise You for being Faithful and True in all things. Amen

October 15
Permission
By Kit Hinkle

> *For God gave us a spirit not of fear*
> *but of power and love and self-control.*
> 2 Timothy 1:7 ESV

You have permission to step out, in a Godly way, to impact this world in a way only you can.

My oldest turned eighteen, and I decided to surprise him with a weekend with his friends at a small villa at the beach—yes, a cold weekend, but who cares? These were really great Christian friends who just wanted to pal around and let my son know they love him.

As I planned it, I had complete confirmation in my heart that it would be fabulous. It would honor God, and He would be right there with me as I chaperoned seven teenagers by myself for an overnight.

… but there were naysayers. I had someone trying to place doubt about it. It stung for only a moment, until I regained my footing and remembered that sometimes the world struggles with seeing a single mom stepping out in life without a husband. I had to remind her that I do have a Husband, and because I walk carefully with Him, and because the families of all the kids who are going trust me, the weekend will go well.

And it did.

The victory is only His. The weekend was beautiful. The teens surprised my eighteen year old by covering him in silly string and then putting him in one of the cars without explanation as we took off for the beach.

We had pizza on the boardwalk. They did a "polar bear" run into the cold ocean waters! They went swimming in a heated pool with fifty degree temperatures outside! They put a sombrero on his head and I served up a Tex-Mex dinner at the villa. They put on a funny goofy birthday talent stunt for him that had us all laughing, and the boys wrestled and goofed around the villa for the evening. They watched a movie and then crashed.

I served up eggs and bacon before sunrise, and they held their own church "service" by the ocean. They played backgammon and a hysterical teenage party game. We drove into Charleston and shopped at the markets. Then we stopped at a Zaxby's along the way home, and they finished the weekend with a Bible study on Luke 9.

Did I need permission from the naysayers? No.

I get my permission from the Lord.

Listen to Him and use the gifts He gave you to impact the world around you. I'm so grateful these seven teens got to experience God's grace in spiritually sound friendships during a weekend that just may have been defining in their young Christian walk.

Dear Lord, I pray I will have stories to share about listening and acting on Your instructions in spite of worldly opinions. You alone decide what I can accomplish! Give me assurance that Your permission is all I need. Amen

October 16
Reluctant Hero
By Rene Zonner

> *He gives strength to the weary*
> *and increases the power of the weak.*
> *Isaiah 40:29 NIV*

"It's a bird--it's a plane--no, it's Super Widow!" Maybe that is a little over the top. But it's what I feel I have to live up to at times.

Well-meaning friends say things like, "You're so strong!" or "I don't know how you do it all!" and "I really admire you!" One even went so far as to say I was her "hero". What in the world was she thinking?

I'm not a hero. Don't they all see the days when I can barely hold it together? What about those times when I forget something important, simply because I can't squeeze one more thing into this overloaded brain? Or those nights as I sit in my quiet home after all the kids go to bed, crying out for God to rescue me-- it's too much and I feel like I'm drowning?

The Oxford Dictionary defines hero as "a person, typically a man, who is admired or idealized for courage, outstanding achievements or noble qualities".

Well, maybe there is a little something to this hero thing after all.

I would say, at best, I am a reluctant hero.

I certainly didn't ask to be a widow at the age of 40. Never imagining I would be a single mom to three school age children, many days I feel like an alien from the planet Widowhood attempting to live in a world of "complete" families.

But you know what? Batman didn't asked to be orphaned as a child. Spiderman never asked to be bit by a radioactive spider. Superman was an alien refugee from the planet Krypton. Heroes don't ask to be heroes, it just happens.

C.S. Lewis is quoted as saying, "Hardship often prepares an ordinary person for an extraordinary destiny."

I didn't ask for this journey, but it is the one God gave me. So, if I have to walk this road, I want to make sure something good comes from it. I want God to take my story and use it for something extraordinary.

I want to touch lives, to change lives while walking this path. Trust me, I will make mistakes. There will be days when it all feels too hard. There will be days I fail. It's those days I must remember-- real heroes aren't perfect.

So, if friends, family, and even strangers want to admire me? That's okay. For you see, in my world, I am doing some extraordinary things.

I am doing the work of two parents all by myself.

I take care of my home, lead a mom's ministry at my church, and run a business.

I am moving forward courageously when I really wish I could just go back to my old life.

I am facing my fear of an unknown future and not backing down.

I am stronger than I was before my husband died.

I am a hero.

Unlike the heroes in movies and comic books, I thankfully don't have to depend on my own strength or super powers to do these things. I have the power of Christ working in me.

Whenever others look at me and see courage, strength, or some other quality they admire, it's not me they see, it's Jesus Christ. Philippians 4:13 states, "I can do all things through Christ who strengthens me."

There is no way I could travel this journey without the Spirit bubbling up inside of me. If in living out this so-called heroic life I am able to point others to Jesus, bringing out the hero in them, then I say bring it on!

Dear sisters, I encourage you to embrace your inner hero. Recognize that you are doing something heroic in living through the death of your husband.

See the strong person you are becoming as you travel this journey. Don't try and do it in your own strength. Draw on the power of the Holy Spirit. Walk closely with Jesus and let Him be what strengthens you.

Don't be afraid of your weaknesses and don't

get discouraged when it all feels like too much.

Remember Paul? In 2 Corinthians 12:9, he shares how he pleaded with the Lord to take away the thorn in his flesh but the response was, "My grace is sufficient for you, for My power is made perfect in weakness." Paul then says he will "boast all the more gladly about my weaknesses, so that Christ's power may rest on me".

When you are weak, my friends, through the power of Christ you are strong!

Father, thank You for the power I have in Jesus Christ and the Holy Spirit. I pray I will embrace this power, that I will recognize the strength I have because of You. Remind me it is okay to be weak because that is when Your power is made perfect. When others look at me and what I am doing, let it be Jesus they see. Let my willingness to be a hero for You, bring out the hero in those around me. Amen

October 17
Change of Plans
By Karen Emberlin

For I know the plans I have for you," declares the LORD, "plans to prosper you and not to harm you, plans to give you hope and a future. Then you will call on me and come and pray to me, and I will listen to you. You will seek me and find me when you seek me with all your heart.
Jeremiah 29:11-13 NIV

Just months ago, the hopes, dreams, and plans that my husband and I had were suddenly snatched away from me. I woke one morning to discover my husband, lover, and best friend had "gone home to be with Jesus".

What a shock!!

We had just spent Christmas, our forty-eighth anniversary, and New Year's together! I had no idea that anything was wrong.

In the minutes, hours, days, weeks, and even months that passed, I couldn't begin to understand how I could manage without him, much less making "plans" for the future. I depended on him for everything from driving me to helping me daily monitor my "brittle" diabetes. He never complained and was always there for me! We had the joy of raising a daughter and a son, were blessed with four grandchildren, and experienced the adventures of "working for ourselves" for over thirty years, spending everyday together. I felt as though part of me was taken away!

I had to "change plans"! And more drastically than most new widows. With my diabetes, I did not want to stay alone. My family is spread over four states, neither in which I lived.

So two weeks after losing my husband, I sorted our "stuff" and moved several hundred miles away with only a fraction of my belongings.

It was a comfort to be with grandchildren in my daughter's home, but not really the life I wanted. I missed getting out each day, the business contacts we had, and our church friends and activities. I had this "tug" in my heart to find some of these things again but did not know how and still did not know what "plans" God would have for me.

So, "change of plans" again!

Someone suggested a "retirement" center. I cringed. Then the Lord began to "flip" that idea around and helped me understand how this "Village" offers me "people, support, relief, hope, and opportunities to serve Him". He again blessed me by working out many details that looked impossible. I move into my new home in just a couple of weeks.

God's plans for my husband were to take him "home" - even though I still don't know exactly what all His plans for me hold, I know I'm seeking the Lord in a deeper way than ever before and am looking forward not only to my new home at the retirement village, but to my heavenly home.

A previous pastor wrote to me, "The Bible assures us that if the Lord created the heavens and earth in a matter of days, His preparation for us in heaven over the past two thousand years will be beyond what we could ever imagine. This is our glorious hope! The prospect of seeing a dearly loved one in the future keeps this hope alive in the present."

The days are lonely on this "journey" and I miss my husband very much. I don't think the "hole in my heart" will ever go away. I am thankful that my husband's home-going was peaceful and am very thankful for the forty-eight years of love we shared. God is faithful and I am ready to focus on the next step of His "plan" for me.

Rest in the Lord; wait patiently for Him to act.
Psalm 37:7 (Living Bible)

October 18
Joy Comes in the Mourning
By Nancy Howell

I will praise you, Lord,
because you rescued me.
You did not let my enemies laugh at me.
Lord, my God, I prayed to you,
and you healed me.
You lifted me out of the grave;
you spared me from going down to the place of the dead.
Sing praises to the Lord, you who belong to him;
praise his holy name.
His anger lasts only a moment,
but his kindness lasts for a lifetime.
Crying may last for a night,
*but **joy comes in the morning.***
Psalm 30:1-5 NCV

I'm a Southern girl and proud of it. Raised in a small congregation, I became church pianist at age twelve.

I held that job for thirteen years, until I married my best friend and he whisked me away first to Maryland, then on to Texas.

I cut my teeth on gospel music. Groups such as the Blackwood Brothers, the Stamps, the Gaithers, and others were popular, and I played their songs for offertory many Sunday mornings.

The second twenty-five years of my life have passed, and I don't listen to gospel music anymore. Those old familiar four-part harmonies never even cross my mind. I listen to an eclectic mix of contemporary Christian and classic Rock.

So, imagine my surprise, as somewhat familiar words, and a tune I half-way remember, began playing through my head on a continuous feed two days.

Holidays are a time of reflection for me, always have been. Certain holidays were quickly approaching. And, unlike last year, I wasn't dreading them. Don't get me wrong, I wasn't particularly looking forward to it. My late husband loved the holidays and was the biggest kid in the family.

Somehow, though, I knew it would be okay.

I had been at my seasonal job, at a local jewelry store, helping customers (especially men on last-minute shopping missions) pick out gifts for their wives-moms-girlfriends.

Heading home for the day, I felt unusually chipper. I started to feel a sensation deep within my gut, which quickly spread throughout my whole body, reaching even my fingertips and toes.

At first, I wasn't sure what it was. The old feeling was familiar, but it had been so very long since it had been inside me. And, sitting at a stop light, as a silly smile crept across my face, I solved the mystery.

I was experiencing JOY.

There was *joy* in my life again. The tears flowed and I laughed out loud to God.

And the chorus of the Bill Gaither gospel song played through my mind, more loudly and more clearly than the contemporary Christian music, which was simultaneously playing in my car.

"Hold on my child, Joy comes in the morning..."

Joy.

Joy had come.

To me.

I couldn't stop praising God as I travelled the short distance home. Simultaneously laughing and crying, I knew in that moment that I was well on my way to being healed.

Dear sisters, if God can do this for me, I am certain He can do the same for you.

Time is not the healer in a widow's journey, although time can help you look at circumstances more clearly. **GOD is the consummate healer in a grief journey.**

Lay it all out on the table for Him. Hold nothing back. God knows all of your faults, your deepest hidden secrets...and He loves you in spite of them.

He has your name written in the palm of His hand.

Let Him hold **your** hand. Let Him **carry you** whenever you cannot walk on your own. Allow others to help you. You have friends that don't know what to do for you. Do them a favor and tell them what you need.

Keep the faith.

And there will come a day, maybe tomorrow, or six months, or seventeen months from now, when you will tingle from head to toe with unexplained joy.

God has promised it.

In Psalm 30, read again the verbs describing God: he **rescues.** He **heals.** He **lifts** you out of the grave. He **spares** you. He **changes** sorrow into dancing. He **clothes** you in happiness.

How lucky are we? Our God doesn't sit on the sidelines. He is a God of action. Call out to Him. He will listen:

I called to you, Lord,
and asked you to have mercy on me.
I said, "What good will it do if I die
or if I go down to the grave?
Dust cannot praise you;
it cannot speak about your truth.
Lord, hear me and have mercy on me.
Lord, help me."
You changed my sorrow into dancing.
You took away my clothes of sadness,
and clothed me in happiness.
I will sing to you and not be silent.
Lord, my God, I will praise you forever.
                        Psalm 30:8-12 NCV

*Heavenly Father, I come in search of healing. Remind me that seeking Your face through prayer and meditation will help me figure out my next chapter in life. Wipe my tears when they drip from my chin. Pick me up and dust me off. Hold me tightly whenever I long to be held by arms belonging to loved ones, now praising You up in heaven. Please give me glimpses of joy and laughter along the way. And no matter how dark the night, always remind me that dawn is coming. It **always** comes. In Your Son Jesus' name, Amen.*

Hold on, my friends. Joy comes in the "mourning."

The darkest hour means that dawn is just in sight.

October 19
The Danger of Pride
By Rene Zonner

> *Pride goes before destruction,*
> *a haughty spirit before a fall.*
> *Proverbs 16:18 NIV*

Pride, Loftiness, Egotism, Arrogance

These aren't words typically associated with a grieving widow. A significant loss, such as the one we have all suffered, has a tendency to ground you and keep you from thinking too highly of yourself.

What about these words?

Self-importance, self-regard, self-absorption

Hmmm, these words are starting to hit a little too close to home.

Recently, I heard pride described as being obsessed with yourself. This obsession can take the form of thinking you are amazing and something more special than others. Okay, that makes sense to me. I feel like I'm pretty good at avoiding that trap. But then, it went on to say that pride can also be an obsession with how unhappy you are or how bad your life is. Ouch! Now we are getting a little too close for comfort.

As a widow I have been dealt a pretty hard blow in life. We all know losing your spouse is just hard. It doesn't matter if you knew it was coming or if it happened unexpectedly. It still hurts whether you were married for a short time or lifetime. Widowhood is a hard lot in life. No one is going to fault me for having bad days or for being sad.

In those early days, especially, it was hard to

grasp that not everyone's world had stopped like mine had. It was hard to understand that not everyone was thinking of John constantly or lamenting over what we lost, every minute of the day. To say that I was self-absorbed is an understatement but, it's perfectly normal and okay…for a season.

But if I am honest with myself, there came a time when normal grief turned into just plain wallowing. I reached a point when my misery had become an obsession. Some days the little extra attention I got for being down felt good to my lonely soul. There were times when the pity party was just easier than "putting on my big girl pants". When obsessing over what I had lost was more comfortable than the hard work it took to move forward.

There is danger in this type of obsession, my friends. When we become self-absorbed with ourselves, whether it's our greatness or our misery, we are being prideful and the Bible tells us that pride will lead to our destruction.

But even more than that, Jesus tells us that He came so that we might have life and have it to the abundance (John 10:10). God doesn't want us stuck in pain and hurt and grief. He wants to bestow on those that grieve a crown of beauty rather than ashes (Isaiah 61:2-3). So when I refuse to let go of the pain, I am basically saying to God, "I know better than You how to deal with this loss."

Friends, we all grieve at a different pace. My journey is not going to be the same as yours. Some of you came to this realization quicker than I did and others will need a whole lot more time than me. That's okay. For me, it's about letting God examine my heart. It's asking Him if I am stuck in grief or if I what I'm feeling is a normal part of the healing journey.

Don't fall into the trap of comparing where you are to my journey or anyone else's. But do remember this, Ecclesiastes 3:4 says, "There is a time to weep and a time to laugh; a time to mourn and a time to dance." Don't miss out on your time to laugh and dance because it's easier and more comfortable to weep and mourn. When you're ready, God will prompt your heart and you will know that it's time.

Don't let the enemy steal, kill and destroy the things God so wants for you to know in Him. At the right time, take the step towards the joy He so abundantly bestows when we allow Him to do so.

Father God, help me take the steps toward joy today. I do not want to fall in the trap of comparing or wallowing. Reveal to me where I am obsessed with self-pity or unhappiness. Following You is my greatest desire, Lord. Amen

October 20
Step By Step
By Sheryl Pepple

The Lord makes firm the steps of the one who delights in him;
though he may stumble, he will not fall,
for the Lord upholds him with his hand.
Psalm 37:23-24 NIV

We take a few steps and then we forget we can walk...

Recently I had an opportunity to spend the

day with my grandson. Earlier in the week, he had taken those precious first steps. As soon as I saw the video, I started dreaming about what was yet to come, his walking to me to be scooped up in a big Nana hug, walking on the beach with him before we go snorkeling together, someday watching him walk his beautiful young bride down the aisle. We have so many things to look forward to. But (imagine the sound of the rewind button) we were not there yet.

My daughter did a good job of setting my expectations before I arrived at their house, reminding me that he had just taken a couple of steps earlier in the week but none since then. Grandson and I started the day with a quick diaper change, followed by floor time to play with his toys. I took a few minutes to pick out his clothes and then sat on the floor to dress him. Busily digging for toys in his toy box, he saw me sit down and immediately walked over to me. No chance to build up the anticipation, no fanfare or thought, he just walked over to me. And then for the next two days he crawled, everywhere he went.

Crawling, that's what I have been doing this week. My slump began when I started feeling rundown. It never ceases to amaze me how when I am physically not feeling well, the emotions seize the opportunity to take over. I miss my husband, I am tired of hurting, I want to go back to the way things were, I don't want to do this anymore…those all too familiar feelings of despair.

God pulled me out of the pit of despair by reminding me of my grandson's first steps and how those first steps are similar to the first steps in our grief journey. We often take those first steps with no anticipation, fanfare, or thought. And many times we want to go right back to crawling. We are afraid, unsure, and we don't want to fall.

But God sees the whole picture. He knows that in order to for us to accomplish His purposes we have to take those first steps, and then the next ones, and the ones after that. Not every step is easy, and sometimes we will stumble and get hurt, but step by step, we will continue the journey. We will run into the arms of our Father and get the best hug ever. We will have new adventures and new life events. We will know the great *I Am* in ways we could have never known Him before. My dear sisters, there is so much yet to come. We need to remind each other to keep walking.

Dear Heavenly Father, Thank You so much for teaching me to walk, for making my steps firm, for holding me in Your hand. Thank You for giving me the endurance and the encouragement to complete this journey. Father, please help me love, encourage, and strengthen others, that the world may see You in all that I say and do, each step of the way. I love You, Father, and I walk this journey for Your glory. Amen.

October 21
I Choose, Do You?
By Leah Stirewalt

I heard a comic once say that it's not people who kill the squirrel as it scurries across the street in front of a car, only to suddenly make a faulty decision to reverse and go the other way. Suddenly, it chooses to reverse again, turning to face the ultimate...SMACK!

No – it's not the person or the car that killed the squirrel. It was indecision. If the squirrel would have just kept running forward, it might have evaded the coming car and its ultimate death. Or maybe if the squirrel had stopped in its tracks, the car could have straddled it or veered around it. Instead...it scampered back and forth trying to decide what to do until it was too late.

I am the squirrel. I find myself very indecisive these days – or unable to make decisions at all. In studying up on this journey of grief, I realize that's perfectly normal for widows. I realize this particular dilemma will fade, and my ability to make decisions (or make them more quickly) will return.

There is one choice that I have decisively chosen to make, in spite of my pain...**I choose to get well!**

Much like the invalid of thirty-eight years in the book of John, when Jesus asked him, *"Do you want to get well?"*

And how did the invalid respond? With an excuse, *"Sir...I have no one to help me into the pool when the water is stirred. While I am trying to get in, someone else goes down ahead of me."*

But Jesus didn't stop there. He didn't say, "I'm so sorry. That's such a shame. Maybe I can 'stop traffic' long enough for you to get down into the water." Rather, Jesus the Healer said to him, *"Get up! Pick up your mat and walk."*

And what happened next? Scripture tells

us, *"At once the man was cured; he picked up his mat and walked."*

The man made a decision. He chose to do what Jesus asked him to do – without hesitation – and he found his healing.

What does that look like for a widow in desperate need of healing from a broken heart, among other things?

In the early days...it might look like this...

When we feel like we can't get out of bed...we CHOOSE to move locations, maybe just to the couch.

When we don't feel like praying...we CHOOSE to utter one simple prayer, "Lord, please help me!"

When we don't want to read the Word...we CHOOSE to open up the book of Psalms and simply read the first one.

When we don't feel like socializing...we CHOOSE to return to church to allow God to love on us through other people. And, if we're not loved on in that church, we CHOOSE another.

When we don't think we can eat even a morsel...we CHOOSE to make and eat a piece of dry toast.

A few months or weeks down the road...it might look like this...

When we feel that we need help...we CHOOSE to seek the advice of a grief counselor, attend a grief program, or see a medical doctor.

When we can't seem to muster up enough energy to do the basics around the house...we CHOOSE to share our struggle with a close friend or family member who can help us.

When we begin to express anger towards our beloved husband…we CHOOSE to write him a letter expressing the pain, anger, and full emotion completely.

In the later months or years…it might look like this…

When our healing seems to be in full swing…we CHOOSE to open our hearts to another grieving widow that needs to know she's not alone.

When we feel the loneliness set in again…we CHOOSE to spend time with friends and not live as a hermit.

If/when we ever feel the desire to date once again…we CHOOSE to take the matter to the Lord for His decision to be made for us.

Making the decision to be well is the first step. It may take us months or years to get there, but admitting that we want to be well, and then opening our hearts to allow God to work on us from the inside out is one of the most decisive choices we can make for ourselves as widows.

Not only will we benefit from that choice, but our children, grandchildren, parents, siblings, closest friends, co-workers, neighbors, and anyone else we interact with will also reap huge blessings from that initial decision for healing.

And most importantly…when we realize all that God has done for us through this most difficult journey…we CHOOSE to give Him glory!

And so…my sweet widow friends, what choice is God asking you to make today?

October 22
A Call For Community
By Katie Oldham

What if you don't have to do this alone?
I've trained myself to put one foot in front of the other and run on adrenaline. Tell this lady to '*just do her best and forget the rest*' and I'll offer a sincere smile, nodding, yet dismissing the wisdom in your words.

HELP: A four letter word in my personal pocket dictionary defined as 'weakness'. Truth is, I innocently just want to make my own way under the radar, not coming across as a nuisance or inadequate.

So, me ask for help? Not even when widowhood wears me so thin I can hardly withstand the wind. Not when single motherhood has my knees hitting the floor in frustration.

But this stops me short: Ecclesiastes 4: 9-12. I'd glossed over it before but the timing wasn't right. Now it hits me square in the stubborn, seemingly self-sufficient head.

Two are better than one, because they have a good return for their labor: If either of them falls down, one can help the other up. But pity anyone who falls and has no one to help them up! Also if two lie down together, they will keep warm. But how can one keep warm alone? Though one may be overpowered, two can defend themselves. A chord of three strands is not quickly broken. (NIV)

Lord, I just want to serve You! But, maybe servant-hood doesn't mean living without need in my own life….

Read again those Biblical words. Are you underline convicted like I or underline comforted by the sense of **community**?

I long for the former, a life alongside **Christian comrades supporting each other in community**. So, I'm aiming to soften my solitary ways.

I'm calling out more often, learning to accept assistance. When I'm simply worn thin not needing a hand, there's warmth just in knowing someone's there to *pick me up, encourage me, to offer perspective or validation.*

God says we were made for companionship…Christian companionship. I've often avoided the idea because it reminds me of the love I lost when my husband left for heaven. But I'm certain romantic love isn't what God meant here: *'A cord of three strands is not quickly broken.'*

He wants us to work together, hold up, hold on to and defend each other. Who am I to go against that Godly grain?!

Community. Companionship. It comes at a cost but there's such value in vulnerability!

Jesus formed churches to gather in worship, Each time we lean into a Christian community we feel a sense of *inclusion*.

But it's not only inclusion we need. As women and moms working hard, we require validation, too.

Why not tip toe off our pedestals to faithfully fill our needs through the hands of helpers God gave us? Rather than a nuisance, it offers others opportunity to obey God's command to serve one another.

Through community, we are *held up and held accountable*. We give and receive, support and seek.

I now know I wasn't made to do 'life' alone. I value the village God built around my little family.

I use my time and talents but without tapping myself out. When I white knuckle the wheel of over-commitment I easily fall further from God, even when I'm giving!

Do you feel it, too? In the stress of doing everything alone do you become distracted from the life He wants you to live, losing touch with what's important?

Take it from a former overly independent martyr (I mean mother!): Stay close to a Christian community. Spiritually, occupationally and even at home, you're not alone.

Lord God, help me go forth and build a world of encouragers, Lord lovers and Christian community. Help me support others and not criticize. And help me allow others to help me as they serve You. Amen

October 23
I Really Just Want...
By Erika Graham

Casting all your care on Him, because He cares for you.
Be of sober spirit, be on the alert.
Your adversary, the devil, prowls around like a roaring lion,
seeking someone to devour.

But resist him, firm in your faith...
1 Peter 5:7-9 NIV

"I really just want my daddy...I miss him!" One of my sweet boys proclaimed through tears.

On one holiday night, as our day of celebration with a houseful of family was waning, my daughter came to tell me one of my boys was sobbing in his bed with the covers over his head. As I walked upstairs, I prayed that God would give me words filled with love, comfort, and truth for whatever made him so upset.

I entered and reached under the covers to caress his forehead. After a few minutes he pulled the covers down, and with tears streaming, his words thrust us into our toughest moment; when one of my kids really just WANTS his daddy and there's nothing I can do.

You see, my husband was a twin, and even though they look different and act differently, he and his brother sounded SO much alike.

When we were dating in high school, I'd call his house and start blabbering away. Sometimes it would be several minutes before I would be told Scott wasn't even home! But I did it over and over. It is a wonderful memory, which made hearing his brother's voice so very hard after Scott's death. But now I realize what a special blessing and privilege it is that not many get.

I forget though, as my kids are processing their grief, it can be different. With my brother-in-law here, my son had a tangible reminder, all day long, that he can never see or hear his daddy in person again. After a while, it was too much for him, so he escaped to his room, pulled the covers over his head, and cried.

How many times do my kids cry out for their father? Far too many to count!

How many times do I cry out for my Father to help us, to give me guidance? Even more!

But unlike my kids cries for their earthly daddy, there is a Father in Heaven that hears AND answers me.

Yet, sometimes I cry out to God and hear an imitator instead, and I am fooled by that imitator, like I was so many times by my husband and his brother back in high school.

The Bible is clear; Satan is the greatest imitator of all. He prowls around looking to speak lies to us and steal us from our true Father.

As my son and I talked about his daddy and the things we love and miss the most, it was a valuable reminder for me of how important it is to continuously be filling myself up with God's voice, through His Word and His promises to me. My grief makes me weak and, like my son, an easy target for my emotions and pain to get the better of me. In my weakness, Satan can get in and devour me.

As I reflected and went on my knees before the Lord later that night, He revealed how important it is for me to turn to Him, the true Healer, each and every day. I need to turn my children over to His care as well, trusting He will be everything they need in this journey, praying they will never be fooled by the imitator either.

Father, protect me from Satan's snares as I travel this grief road. It's so hard at times to stay focused on You and so easy to wallow in my pain and sadness. But Your promises are the real deal. Meet our needs Lord, heal my heart, and protect my mind. Help me to continually renew my desire to seek You and to turn my grief and my children's grief over to You, to never be fooled by the imitations, but to resist and stand firm in YOU. Amen

October 24
Call Me "Mara"
By Sherry Rickard

And she said unto them,
Call me not Naomi, call me "Mara";
*for the Almighty hath dealt very **bitterly** with me.*
Ruth 1:20 KJV

I am "Mara"! I can relate to this Bible reference to Naomi, who lost her husband and her two sons, and just wanted her neighbors to call her by her new name, Mara. Take a few minutes to read her story in the Old Testament book of Ruth if you want to.

I try to laugh every day and try to keep my negativity (bitterness) from getting the best of me. When someone has an idea (including me), I have the ability within moments to (in my head) come up with several reasons that idea should never see the light of day. When I hear news (good or bad), I immediately have several thoughts about how the good can turn bad and the bad can turn to worse. I fight it all day, every day.

The only way I can combat my natural tendency to do this is to think of at least one positive thing for each negative thing that comes to mind. Over the years of making myself do this; I have been able to turn the tide of my natural tendency towards bitterness into a studied habit of positive thoughts and actions.

Widowhood has not made this natural tendency towards bitterness easier. Bitterness is an emotion that I fight against almost every day since my Bill's home-going, or promotion, as I like to call it. Some days it just oozes from my pores and during others it is a shadow in the room that I can refuse to step into.

On the days it seeps from me, I find myself just wanting to wallow in my anger and pick fights on innocent victims. People who are driving on the road with me…my pets…my daughter…my friends. Thankfully, these days are few and far between.

I am several years down this road called Grief. I still have days of sadness and loneliness that make me bitter sometimes. I wanted to walk this journey fast and get through it and be healed and move on. I don't want it to take time.

I want to be loved again. I want to go to a restaurant and ask for a table for two in a quiet corner to just spend time with someone special. I want back-up when I have to discipline my teenager – a voice louder than mine that reminds her to "respect your mother and my wife". I want to go on vacation and let my left hand drop from my lounge chair by the pool only to be caught by a strong, right hand and held. I am bitter…"Mara".

Then my loving Savior whispers into my

heart, "I am here and I love you!" I am reminded that Christ chose me; not at my best, but my worst. He died for me for the sole purpose that I could spend eternity with Him because He wants me.

For some strange reason, He needs me to walk this journey. He doesn't want me to be sad, angry or bitter. He wants me to take those emotions off like heavy coats and leave them with Him. He wants me to lean on Him for being wholly loved; to discipline my daughter and know He will lovingly guide her because she has Him in her heart too; and to walk the beach while on vacation sharing time with Him.

When I lean on Him, everything just seems to fall into focus. My loneliness slips away; my sadness diminishes; my heart is full; peace is with me; contentment is part of my wardrobe; and everything is ok. I am even ok with being asked to walk this journey and some days, people see Christ in me and say I am inspiring. (I know this is not me, but Christ in me.)

These are the days when that bitterness is a shadow that I don't step into. These are the days when "Mara" ("bitter") is not my name. These are the days that I am surrendered and lay my head down at night feeling accomplished in Christ with a smile on my face.

I'm not there yet, but I am still on the road. And it is on this road that I am finding that "Mara" is getting further and further behind me and the name "Joy" is one I wear when I am surrendered and Christ is shining through me.

I cannot encourage you enough to leave "Mara" behind and choose to be "Joy". "Mara" is a season, not a destination. "Joy" is a destination that we are all working towards.

Dear Lord, I am so thankful You allow me to have my "Mara" moments and love me through them. I am so thankful that You bring me into Joy-filled moments. I cannot think of a more fulfilling love than the love I have in You. Thank You for being with me on this journey and may I have more Joy moments in You. I love You! Amen

October 25
Big Plans
By Kit Hinkle

> *Then the LORD said to Satan,*
> *"Have you considered my servant Job?*
> *There is no one on earth like him;*
> *he is blameless and upright,*
> *a man who fears God and shuns evil.*
>
> *Job 1:8 NIV*

I love this verse. It gives me a peek into a conversation God had with Satan over a man named Job. Job is being put into a big story but he never gets told any details and doesn't get to approve of the script ahead of time.

Guess what? You and I are part of a big story and we may never get told the chapter title or even who all the "actors" are in the story.

When you are hurting and wondering why

God would let you go through this circumstance, think of Job, and how he struggled with the same questions, and how throughout the entire book of Job, you know something about Job's situation that he didn't know.

That might help you think about your circumstance differently, like a story, like a book that's about to be written, just as a book was written about Job. Think of what the Author sees in your life--the big picture.

If you trust your Author, like Job trusted God, you will be able to overcome your circumstances.

Job lost everything, but never lost sight of how perfect God is!

Job's friends first listened and prayed over him, but then got impatient and started to ask Job what he did to deserve such calamity in his life.

Job searched himself and couldn't find fault that would warrant such calamity.

Once Job was completely sure he did nothing to deserve what happened, he started to ask God why. But we, as the readers of Job, already know why.

We know, but Job and his friends didn't. The whole time they pondered this situation, they were looking at it while in the battlefield of life---not from above.

But we, as readers, are allowed to see the bigger picture. The writer of Job pulled back the curtain to show us the conversations God had with Satan. Satan approached God and told God, "See, Job over there? I bet he's only following You because he's got it so good. Take away the goodies, and I bet he'll curse You."

God then allowed Satan to have his way with Job…. for the glory of God…

Do you get it, Sister? Job suffered because his suffering became an illustration to the rest of mankind that **we worship and follow the one and only God Almighty, not because of the goodies He gives us, but because of Who He is**! And our worship of Him is not connected to our circumstances.

When Job finally asked God why, God never spelled out to Job the reason why! Why didn't He? How encouraging that would have been to Job!

Why doesn't God tell you why you are having to go through all of these challenges?

Here's perhaps a reason why. If God would have described to Job the conversations He had with Satan over the righteousness of Job, **then Job would have understood and had faith in God because he had knowledge, not true faith.**

Trust God. You don't **know** His purpose, but you can **trust** His purpose.

Rise above the circumstance. He has plans for you--big plans.

October 26
Buddy the Dog and Me
By Elizabeth Dyer

Come to me, all you who are weary and burdened,
and I will give you rest.

Matthew 11:28 NIV

Since adopting a puppy, we have had lots of stories: stories of chewed up shoes and clothes; stories of terrified neighbor children. My favorite stories are the ones that happened as daddy was trying to leave for church after I had already gone early for orchestra. Buddy the Dog would inevitably drag some item out of the garage and wait for daddy to chase him around. Once Buddy dragged out the electric hedge trimmer still in the box and ran wild in the backyard.

This past winter, we had some very cold days (at least for the south!) so Buddy was given more opportunities to stay inside while we were gone. One particular day we were trying to leave to go somewhere and there was Buddy running around the back yard with trash in his mouth. We chased him around like idiots, yelling at him and calling him a bad dog. Nothing worked. Nothing made him drop his garbage so he could be allowed into the warmth of the house. Here is a family dressed in Sunday clothes, chasing a big black dumb dog around the yard **for trash**! It didn't take me long to give in and leave him out. We were initially sad about leaving him outside but that changed after I convinced the kids that it was his stupid choice.

He gave up the opportunity for warmth in order to hold onto his garbage.

When I told the kids that there must be a spiritual application somewhere in this story, one teen said, "God gave us dogs in order to see ourselves." Pretty insightful!

Are there times I have found myself holding

onto the "garbage" of my own way while God is calling me to the warmth and peace of His will? Do you ever find yourself there too? Like Buddy the Dog, we keep running around with our plans rolled up in our mouths. We have ideas, plans, lists, but they aren't what God has in mind for us. It keeps coming down to my will versus His will. Pride versus humility. Accepting His plan for my life, and living that life for His glory and not my own.

I hold onto that garbage and run around the yard! I don't want to let go of it...But I have to let go of it in order to follow God. He doesn't **make** me drop it. He doesn't chase me with a large stick like I may or may not have done with Buddy the Dog. He promises that His yoke is easy. Yokes never give the idea of ease but perhaps we need to stop pulling at the yoke or trying to go where the yoke doesn't fit well.

But never in the sense that "easy" means "without trials". When Jesus told the disciples that they needed to cross the water in a boat and, while they were obeying Jesus, they encountered a storm, they were right where God wanted them.

The Apostle Paul went through a lot of difficulties while following God. I think it has to do more with a humble acceptance that we are right where God wants us to be, right where He can use us to help someone else, right where we can bring glory to Him, right where we totally rely on Him and not ourselves.

So when I look at Buddy the Dog, I ask myself if I am choosing the garbage of my way instead of the warmth of God's will.

Father God, You call us to Yourself. You offer the promise of Your yoke being easy. Guide me today as I follow Your will and not my own. Help me to drop the "garbage" in my life, drop the constant urge to perform for Your love, and just accept the love You offer and the warmth of following Your will. Thank You that You don't force us to follow but that You lovingly hold Your hands out to us. Amen

October 27
A Picture is Worth at Least a Thousand Words
By Liz Anne Wright

Let the redeemed of the Lord tell their story—
those He redeemed from the hand of the foe,
those He gathered from the lands,
from east and west, from north and south.
Psalm 107:2-3 NIV

When we moved into our new house about a year and a half before my husband died, I tried some new decorating ideas. I ditched a lot of my collections and went for a more minimalist approach. That included the area of photographs. I had read once that when decorating your home, personal, family pictures should not be in the living areas. I still follow that philosophy today. Upstairs, there are plenty of pictures. They line the hall, showing our family as it grew and how it has changed since we lost Dad. Downstairs, however, there are not family photos.

But there is one exception.

About a year after their dad died, a dear friend

of mine, who is a professional photographer, took pictures of our family. As it happened, that day I was putting away Dad's military camouflage "utilities". When this friend asked me if I had any special pictures I wanted to take, I thought of those "utilities". Each one of the boys put on their dad's uniform as my friend snapped beautiful memories for each of us.

This picture has become the centerpiece of my dining room for two reasons.

First of all, it is a sweet reminder of my sweet husband – his love of country that prompted him to devote twenty years of his life to protecting it. That is quite a legacy to leave behind…one of which I am very proud.

Secondly, it shows he left an even greater legacy: his children.

Looking at this picture, I can see so much of him in them. One has his dad's twinkle and love of children. Another has his dad's sweetness and devotion to those in his life. The third is the spitting image of young Keith physically, and is quiet like his dad as well. The youngest has the eyes…a different color, yet just as compelling, including long lashes…and has the same recognition Keith had of the importance of touch.

We have a lot of people in our lives today who did not know Keith, did not know the sweet man he was, the dedicated friend, the passionate lover of his Lord. But…by knowing his children, they can see glimpses of him.

To me, this picture represents a window into the life of Keith – what was important to him, who and what he lived for. By being willing to share my boys, I share their dad with all whom I interact…both old and new friends.

As a widow, I am the keeper of a story—my story, the story of my life and of the man I lost. It is my job to keep that story true to him who was here with me and Him who is King of my life. In sharing that story, my husband lives on in an additional way here on earth, but, more importantly, it is an opportunity for me to talk of the glory of our Lord.

Sweet sisters, what pictures do you have of your late husband…in your home and in your head? What legacies did he leave behind? What has Christ done in you and through you since your loss? Those are stories worth sharing!

In the midst of our sorrow, let us not forget to share those boldly with the world. God is sovereign, even in our pain and suffering. That is a picture worth sharing!

Father God, this journey is a hard one…but with You, it is a possible one. Thank You for that. Help me to see Your fingerprints in our lives, even through this grief and sorrow, and help me share with a world that so badly needs it. In Your precious Name, Amen.

October 28
Run, Nancy, Run!
By Nancy Howell

I like to run. If you know me, you know that this activity keeps me centered. It lifts my mood. It raises my endorphin level. It allows time for just me, which is something that is so necessary with all that's swirling around me in the past few months. I know, that to be healthy and ready for the challenges of my new normal life, I have to take time to exercise, to listen to God, to talk with my husband, to commune with the outdoors.

I've always run to music. Classic rock, pop, regular rock, you name it---my playlist runs the spectrum. Since losing my husband, I've run mostly "sans music" (without), feeling like I needed the quiet time to reflect, meditate, and pray.

But I began to miss my tunes, and decided to phase the music back in, a little at a time. If I came across a song that just didn't fit my mood, or made me too sad, I would just skip over it. That's worked pretty well, although I still felt like something was missing from my music library.

Contemporary Christian music is a genre I've never much listened to in the past. Flipping through the radio stations in my car, I might pause and listen to a song or two, but didn't linger long. It sounded nice and I appreciated it, but I didn't take the time to really hear any of the songs. Since losing my husband, I've lingered longer on these stations. As I listened intermittently for several days, I finally began to get it. It's music with a message, and for a girl that enjoys good beats to run to, this may be the start of a beautiful friendship.

So I went on-line and purchased several songs and two albums. I excitedly downloaded them, created a brand-spanking new playlist, and looked forward to running with it for the first time.

All I can say is WOW. It's a good thing I

stuffed tissues in my running vest, because I think I had the most satisfying run in recent memory. Seemed like most every song spoke to me about my current situation.

Now, I know those composers didn't write those songs with only me in mind, even though they sure sounded like it. The more I visit with people about my loss, the more sad stories I hear in return. Whether it's a death, divorce, estrangement, health issues, money issues---the common thread is brokenness. Physically and/or spiritually broken, we all are brothers and sisters, doing the best we can each and every day. Those songs touch on situations in different ways, with varying melodies, but each reminds us there is hope. And we are not alone.

So I ran. And I cried. And I laughed. And as I stopped to survey our lovely "borrow pit" near Lake Wichita, I smiled. There were ducks back on the water. There are GBH's (great blue herons--husband's acronym for them) looking for fish. Folks, this was a cause for celebration. In the hot of summer, that spot was practically dry. Husband fretted because, if it got too low too quickly to salvage any of the fish, he would've moved them to the bigger lake. Hope came in the form of rain and cooler temperatures. Nature adapts, and life moves on.

Isn't that just like us? We go through periods of drought in our spiritual lives. I'm ashamed to admit that while I was married and things were grand, I didn't thirst after the Bible like I should have. I didn't pray as often as I do now. And I didn't listen to Christian music. Amazing. As long as my life was as close to perfect as it has ever been, I kept God at arm's length. I knew He was there, I loved Him, I acknowledged and thanked Him for all that He'd given me. But when the "rubber met the road", and I was left without a leg to stand on, He grabbed hold of me, and has not let me go.

He was there all along, waiting for me to take notice.

For my family, hope came whenever I admitted I couldn't get through this grief alone, and I surrendered everything to God. I'm adapting, with His help and direction. And as a family, we're moving forward.

I'm now listening to a variety of Christian contemporary songs when I run. I'm not abandoning the old tunes, they have their place. But for the foreseeable future, I'm sticking with the ones that give me hope.

October 29
It's Over
By Leah Stirewalt

Nineteen months to the day later, a signature, and a check for court costs, and it was over! Yesterday officially marked the "closing" of my late husband's estate. I say "estate" loosely. That's the just the probate term for it, but in all honesty, it should have been cut and dry and over with long before now, but there was an attorney turnover that slowed the process down a bit.

For me, the last nineteen months have been the most drastically changed of my entire forty years.

I've been in the deepest of valleys. I've sunken into pits that felt bottomless at times. I've seen me at my worst, and I've been pleasantly surprised at my behavior at other times. I've watched God pour out His unending love on me through His children and through those that mock His name and yet call me friend. I've witnessed miracle after miracle in my life following my husband's "disappearance", suicide, and the discovery of his lifeless body. The biggest miracle? My own healing.

And yet…a simple signature on a document to go to the courthouse, and it's over. Or is it?

For me, the deep pain is over…and yet…some recollection will trigger a flow of tears at other times.

For me, I've been able to move on in life…and yet…someone will mention the word "suicide", and I'll tense up.

For me, I've been able to walk with others down their own Grief Road…and yet…there are times I still send out a text or an email asking for someone to pray me through a rough morning.

For me, I've witnessed God's deep healing in my life…and yet…I've come to realize that grief healing does not always take the form of a one-time event. It might take a lifetime for some (for most).

My precious friend and A Widow's Might sister put it this way in an email to me, "I prayed that with the closing of the estate… there is also a closure in your heart. That our faithful Lord will seal everything He has done over the past year and a half and allow you to place it all on a box on a shelf until He wants you to use it again for His glory. Whether that is daily or occasionally is up to Him."

I loved that! That is a beautiful picture of the VERY thing God has done and, I trust, will continue to do.

He blessed with me a deep, quick, miraculous healing. I have no doubt that for many, it doesn't happen that way. I grieved hard, openly, and faced it head-on. I didn't want to feel that type of pain forever. And the day came…last January actually…where I felt He sealed it all and placed it on a shelf to be opened again only at His choosing. And…He does open the box occasionally…

He opens it to remind me of what He did for me so that I can encourage others going through similar pain.

He opens it to remind me of how deep I hurt so that I can empathize with others fresh on the grief journey.

He opens it to remind me of how far He's brought me when I feel as if His presence isn't quite as near.

He opens it to remind me of the One that is in complete control of my life, even when it doesn't feel that way.

So, while yesterday was the "end" of a season (paperwork speaking), it was only the beginning in the plans God has for me. And…when it comes right down to it…it's not about me anyway. All of it…pain, joy, gladness, mourning, LIFE…it's All for His glory!

Not to us, O LORD, not to us, but to your name give glory,
for the sake of your steadfast love and your faithfulness!
Psalm 115:1, ESV

October 30
Releasing the Patterns of Self Doubt
By Kit Hinkle

*But while everyone was sleeping,
his enemy came and sowed weeds among the wheat,
and went away.*
Matthew 13:25 NIV

Sometimes the weeds the enemy sows are patterns of anxious thoughts.

They start by a valid concern--in our case--the loss--how will we manage without him? Or a worry over finances or your children. But the enemy's seeds start to grow when we hold on to the patterns of anxious thinking beyond where they are useful.

I remember finding myself in a pattern of anxious thinking after a year-long struggle to sell my home. I had four children at the time under the age of six. I kept my home flawlessly clean for showings— eighty-five showings! Can you imagine scrubbing floors and baseboards and staging the furniture perfectly eighty-five times? All the while, toddlers and babies crawled about my feet and preschoolers tugging at my hem.

The constant cycle of adrenaline—clean the house, show the house, wait in anticipation, receive disappointing news, get the call for the next showing—left me repeating a pattern of anxious thoughts that led to a habit.

Once the house sold, the crisis was over. I

figured no more anxiety, right? Wrong. My mind was so used to the pattern of anxiety repeating itself that it looked for something else to put in place of the house selling anxiety. I repeated the emotional cycle with everything from waiting for news on a medical test to waiting to hear from a friend who was deciding whether the book club I invited her to join was a good fit for her.

Because the cycle of emotions were so practiced, I found even a decision over a book club brought the most ridiculous level of anxiety. In noticing it, I identified it as a habit.

You can do the same with your tears. Just observe yourself as you cry. Notice whether the tears are cleansing you or digging you deeper into sadness.

Sometimes we can be tricked into mixing up cleansing tears of grief with tears of self-pity and self-doubt, fed by whispered lies from the enemy.

Only you and the Lord know if your pattern of grieving and bouts of tears have tipped beyond a healthy level. If you find you might have developed a habit, don't feel alone. It's a common experience among those who've been through difficult events in their lives.

Turn instead to new patterns of thinking. Begin with the Word.

> *Blessed are those who have learned to acclaim you,*
> *who walk in the light of your presence, Lord.*
> *They rejoice in your name all day long;*
> *they celebrate your righteousness.*
> *Psalm 89:15-16 NIV*

One friend gave me great advice for breaking a habit. She told me not to assume you can stop the worry and anxiety on your own strength and overnight. Do the following instead: **When you find yourself in an episode of unhealthy negative thinking, just notice the pattern. Label it.**

I thought her advice was interesting. She didn't put pressure on me that the tears of worry I relied on as a crutch had to stop right away, and that was a relief. She only suggested that I keep the following idea in mind as I obsessed over the sadness: "Oh, I see I'm repeating a habit." She said that the more you learn to recognize the habit without beating yourself up over it, the less power the habit has over you, until eventually, you'll begin to observe your tears as though you were someone watching you in tears—someone loving, like a sister in Christ, looking at you and saying, "It's okay. You're not as alone as you think you are." You can begin to embrace your sadness in an observant way and then step aside and let it dissipate.

She was right. Every time an obsessive thought popped in my head, I could see it as a habit before it took root in my heart and threw me down the road of self-pity. It was my first step into a life of boldness.

Father God, please help me be willing to try this technique. Empower me to master the feelings by holding every thought captive so that nothing holds me back from glorifying You. Amen

October 31
Covered By Grace
By Sheryl Pepple

For all have sinned and fall short of the glory of God,
and are justified freely by his **grace**
through the redemption that came by Christ Jesus.
Romans 3:23-24 NIV

I have been mulling over a question recently: How do we care for our grown children during this loss?

I'd like to share what that has looked like for our family; my personal struggles trying to navigate our family through the grief process and what God is teaching me.

In our situation, my husband's death came as a complete surprise. My husband regularly traveled out of town on business, but stayed home for a doctor's appointment. When his doctor's appointment was finished, he called me and we decided to go out to lunch together before he left for his trip. We had a great lunch and I am grateful that God was in all of the details of that day.

After lunch, I needed to drop him off at a rental car place and was joking with him the entire time, about how I was just going to slow the car down and make him hop out because I was late getting back to work. In an effort to be gracious and supportive, he quickly tried to get out of the car, forgetting to take off his seatbelt, which sent us both into more giggles. Flustered, he almost forgot to kiss me goodbye. I quickly reminded him that I am never

163

in such a hurry that I don't want my kiss. Little did I know how precious that entire exchange was going to be, since it would be the last time I would see him on this side of heaven.

Later that evening, the State Troopers arrived to tell me he had been killed by a drunk driver while he was driving to work.

I really struggled with the question; Could I have been a better parent in guiding our family through the grief process?

My marriage to my husband was a second marriage for both of us. My husband had four adult children who were out of the home when we started dating. Because my husband's kids were grown and lived in different states, it had been hard for me to build a relationship with them. I continue to pray for opportunities to build a stronger relationship with each of them.

Then there are my children, who treasured him in so many ways. My daughters were just four and six years old when Dave and I started to date. He became such an integral part of our family and they have such wonderful memories. I know they miss him so much.

My oldest daughter got married just two years before his death. Last year we experienced the blessing of the birth of her first son. It was in this moment that we started to realize how hard it is when life goes on without our loved one.

Last fall, my youngest daughter graciously offered to go to a wedding with me. She was so sweet and supportive the entire trip, watching out for me, making sure I was having a good time. Sitting at the reception, a moment happened that brought reality crashing in again...The father-daughter dance. One moment my daughter was sitting there having a good time, the next moment she was running to the restroom with tears streaming down her face. Oh, how the grief can sneak up on us so furiously, so quickly.

I have never had a time that was harder to breathe than this time in my life. I've had to breathe, actually take in huge gulps, before I was able to care for my adult kids. It feels selfish to take care of my needs first, but truly I believe it is God's grace. This season in our lives is a crucial time for us to cling to Him for our very breath, just as we would those oxygen masks on the airplanes. **And as He restores us, we will be able to care for our children.** As time and my healing has progressed, God has given me some opportunities to care for them, just as they have cared for me.

He guides us each step of the way. We continue to work together as a family to honor my husband, but even more importantly to honor God by testifying to His grace through this difficult journey. Maybe some days I have been selfish, and others not. I don't really know. What I do know and cling to is: He is sovereign, He is good, He loves me, and we are covered by His Grace through the sacrifice on the cross by His Son, Jesus Christ.

November

November 1
God Sent a Sparrow
By Linda Lint

Not one sparrow is forgotten by God.
Luke 12:6 NIV

I was fully prepared to attend our daughter's college graduation by myself. I was **not** prepared to attend alone.

Going by myself meant I would attend the ceremony, take pictures and then go to the care center to share the experience with my husband.

Going alone meant that just ten hours earlier I had received the dreaded call – he had passed in his sleep.

Sitting in the arena on that Sunday afternoon in May, I was in a fog. I desperately wanted to get up and pace – sitting still was difficult. If I sat still too long, I would begin to cry again – and this was not the place for "those" kind of tears. Mercifully I was flanked on each side by kind women who were present for grandchildren. The usual small talk ensued and, in response to their innocent questions, I had to tell them that my husband had passed just hours before. How kind they were, taking my hand and patting my shoulder – a true blessing. During our conversation we had all noticed a bird flying about in the upper rafters. We paid it little mind, because it is a common occurrence to see such things in large arenas.

Music started, the graduates processed in and sat down, and all was quiet. Then, suddenly, right at my feet was a tiny, female sparrow. She looked up at me, tilted her head and then flew away into the rafters again. How grateful I was for the distraction of this little bird's presence. By focusing on her I could refrain from crying and move my head slightly to watch her – thus relieving my desire to get up and pace.

The little sparrow was respectful during the invocation and speeches and stayed high in the rafters – until there was a break. Each time it was quiet, she would fly down over our daughter's head! She was causing quite a stir among the people around me, for the story had spread about why I was there "alone"; and I had already pointed out where our daughter was sitting.

As each graduate walked across the stage the little sparrow was again very respectful, waiting in the rafters quietly. Then it came our daughter's turn. Our beautiful daughter held herself proudly and received her College Diploma with Magna Cum Laude Honors! And when she returned to her seat that little, tiny sparrow flew down from the rafters directly over her head again!

My husband loved the sparrows in our yard. He fed them regularly and made sure there were plenty of houses (which he made himself) for them. It was no "coincidence" or "accident" that brought that sparrow there to comfort me that Sunday in May three years ago.

No, the sparrow was not my husband as I heard some say. I truly believe that little bird was sent by God Himself to help His newest widow through a most difficult day.

That day I was much like that sparrow – lost and alone in a very big, strange place. In the three years since, I have grown stronger, and have been able to use my wings in ways I never expected – even in a big, strange place called "widowhood". It has not been easy. I do still miss my husband; and, to be honest, I needed to take a break from typing to shed some tears.

Now, I ask this question: "If God is able to guide a lone sparrow to a college graduation ceremony in May, isn't He more than able to guide each of us as we journey down our individual paths of widowhood?"

Dear Father, My love for You has grown and deepened over these days during widowhood. You have shown me in countless ways how valuable I am to You – and I am so grateful. Continue to guide me, Father – I am Your tiny sparrow – so much in need of Your love and care. Amen

November 2
Shifting Sands
By Kit Hinkle

On whom do you lean, sisters? Listen to what God says through Jeremiah:

Cursed is the man who trusts in man and makes flesh his strength, whose heart turns away from the Lord. He is like a shrub in the desert, and shall not see any good come. He shall dwell in the parched places of the wilderness, in an uninhabited salt land.

Blessed is the man who trusts in the Lord, whose trust is the Lord. He is like a tree planted by water, that sends out its roots by the stream, and does not fear when heat comes, for its leaves remain green, and is not anxious in the year of drought, for it does not cease to bear fruit."

Jeremiah 17:5-8 ESV

"Kit, this is so unusual," my friend and mentor told me the other day. "This year has brought you so many clear cut changes in relationships that I have to wonder if God is showing you something."

She's right. I sometimes wonder how I wake every morning and feel the joy of the Lord running through my veins.

Then I remember why.

While the ground has shifted beneath my feet so many times this year, I remain not only standing, but grounded—on the rock I chose to stand on from the start. The Rock of God, not of flesh and man, which are like shifting sands. I wanted to write about it because I'm quite sure many of you have struggled with shifting sands.

And I wanted to inspire you to have hope and joy, and not be bewildered by it all. **Nothing and no one in life remains the same.** Solomon points out in Ecclesiastes that generations come and go and the earth remains the same. He's pointing out that changes will come—sands shift.

Later Solomon goes on to show that you must be **anchored in something deeper than what's in**

the flesh.

So here's a running list.

It's been five years since losing Tom, and the Lord's given me many supports—friends, a local friend, a great church, and a great pastor. And last year, He allowed a sweet man into my life. He's a kind and gentle person who asked me to marry him. He wanted to take on my whole family and love and support us, even financially, for the rest of our lives.

So what was my mentor saying about relationships?

First my friend—it was always a difficult relationship, but still comforting to have while I went through the early signs of grief. I learned this relationship wasn't good for me so I had to learn to detach lovingly in order to focus on raising my kids without that negativity.

Second, a breakup with my fiancé—Friends around me told me God was blessing me for my obedience to Him by matching me with a wealthy man. I shrugged that off because I don't agree with that philosophy—it's not Biblical. God won't give me riches because I obey Him, so that's not why I obey Him. **He will provide, and that's enough to trust**. I fell for my fiancé because of his sweetness and integrity. During the process of planning our lives together I realized the marriage wouldn't have been on solid ground and decided against it. He's a wonderful person, but it takes far more grounded faith and emotional strength than he had to take on four children who wish to place God first in their lives.

But He wasn't done.

Most recently my church community has

changed, shifted. Pastors have moved to other locations or left the ministry. They have been personally supportive and guiding my family for years. Another relationship less accessible for support!

I look at my four boys and ask myself— "Where do I go for support now?" New friends step in, and I engage with them. But I'm carefully choosing them, and carefully choosing how I share and trust in them.

In the Bible verses I've quoted above, Jeremiah is giving the Israelites a clear warning from God **not to trust flesh, but trust Him**.

It's funny how, as each of these changes hit me, I found strength in my relationship with Christ and stood on the Rock and felt strong.

Meanwhile I stay the course—trust the Lord, and focus on what purpose He has placed in my path.

Sisters, I write this for you to help you understand the many changes our relationships will undergo as we walk this widow's journey. The shifting sands you may be experiencing right now are normal. You will find yourself having to re-establish your support network many times over the years, but don't let that jar you too badly. Trust that since God brought our friendships together before widowhood, He will bring it together after widowhood.

November 3
Why Us?
By Erika Graham

My God, my God, why have you forsaken me?
Matthew 27:46 NIV

One of my kids' favorite words as toddlers was "why". Their curious little minds were like sponges, and they eagerly wanted to know the answers to everything. There were times I was so worn by their "whys", I'd count down the minutes until my husband would arrive home from work, so the "why monsters" would turn to him instead.

After my husband committed suicide, I overheard lots of questions from those around me, and I had a great deal of my own deep questions, many centered on my own "why monsters."

I know God could have chosen to change the circumstances of that horrible day, and the days leading up to it. He can do anything! But He didn't, that was hard to accept.

So the questions before God went something like this: Why not protect my husband or us from this hurt and suffering? Why not use this as a powerful testimony in keeping Scott here? Why allow such a horrific thing to occur? Why us?

I can only assume He probably grew as weary as I used to of my kids. But, I wasn't challenging God's authority or denying His power, I was seeking His divine answers and plans for us. I wanted to know why, so I could know how. Because my why questions were followed with how questions such as: How do I move forward? How do I get my children through this? How do I do all that lies ahead without my husband?

I meditated on God's Word because I thought I would find the elaborate answers we all sought. But, the bottom line is that no one, not one, is above pain and suffering, even God himself. He sent His Son who took on sin at the cross and suffered a most unimaginably painful death to pay the price for us. If God allowed His own Son to suffer for THE greatest purpose, then He's going to allow me to as well.

In fact, as a believer, God's Word is clear that, at times, I will suffer in one way or another. (I Peter 2:21)

From the time sin entered the world, until Christ comes again, it's a part of this life. Yet, I can rest assured that my suffering has purpose and is never wasted, even if I really don't like or understand it.

He didn't reveal specific answers to my questions, but He reminded me of His promises and encouraged me to trust His plan and His provision for me.

The questions many of us had were normal. They stemmed from hurt, fear, even anger, and a lack of understanding. In the Bible there are several who cry out to God during their trials, asking the inevitable questions, because the burdens are great and the flesh is weak: The Psalmists ask why, Job asks why, even Jesus at the cross cries out to God the Father as He paid the price for us all, "Why have you forsaken me?"

I realize God may or may not reveal the answers to the questions I have on this side of Heaven, but when I need to I ask. I humbly go before the cross and cry out to God, recognizing His divine authority and accepting His greater purpose and plans for me, choosing to TRUST Him with everything.

Heavenly Father, this world is so hard and my trials can be so tough. I come before You with questions, not out of a place of an arrogant, hard heart but out of a place of humble love and brokenness before You. Father, continue to reveal Your divine plans, go before me, continuing to bring all glory to You. Lord, help me accept what I don't understand, to choose to trust You throughout this journey. Reveal Yourself in ways I could never imagine. Help me seek You and Your answers whenever I am weak and hurting. In Your Matchless Name, Amen

November 4
Who Am I? Why Am I Here?
By Karen Emberlin

It is God himself who has made us what we are
and given us new lives from Christ Jesus;
and long ages ago he planned that we should spend these lives
in helping others.
Ephesians 2:10 Living Bible

      I recently completed two years of this journey called "Widowhood". You would think by now I would be adjusted to this new life and things would be falling into place. Most days are good and I know that I am working my way through the grief process. However, some days I get this paralyzing feeling throughout my entire being and I have to ask myself, "Who am I and why am I here!!"

      The loss of my husband changed my world completely. We were like two peas in a pod, literally together 24/7. I am not the same person I was before God called my husband home, part of me is here, and part of me went with him. I am no longer the wife I was for forty-eight years, I do not live in the same place, not even the same state, my daily activities have changed, the people I spend time with are different, I have new responsibilities, and the list goes on!!

So, Who Am I???

When those lonely times happen and I am able to get past the waves of grief that want to overtake me, I am reminded that God knows who I am and even cares enough about me to know my name! He knows my hurt and wants to calm the waves when they roll in. He knew me before I was born and is fully aware of the length of my days. He also knew I would face this journey of widowhood!

So, if He knows who I am and cares so much for me, why am I here, what does He want me to do?

One night as I struggled with all of the changes that were happening in my life, I received some words of wisdom from a dear friend who reminded me that we are not put in the world to be happy. God places us here to make an impact. I do believe we are here on earth to honor God, to know Him, and to share the benefits of our experience with others here on earth so we can ultimately spend eternity in Heaven and be reunited with our loved ones!

In order to make an impact for Him, I must move forward. As much as I would like, I cannot remain where I am, and I cannot go back. I can remember the years my husband and I shared together, I can cherish our memories, and I can keep them deep within my heart, forever! However, I need to focus on what is before me and how I am going to get there. In Philippians 3:13 -14, Paul was focused on the goal –

I'm not saying that I have this all together, that I have it made. But I am well on my way, reaching out for Christ, who has so wondrously reached out for me. Friends, don't get me wrong: By no means do I count myself an expert in all of this, but I've got my eye on the goal, where God is beckoning us onward—to Jesus. I'm off and running, and I'm not turning back.(The Message)

Sometimes when it's hard to look forward and it's still painful to look back, I know I have to look to the Father and keep my eyes on Him. If I am to make an impact for Him, even through this time of grief in my life, I know I must walk humbly with Him and trust Him for all He has for me!

My prayer each day is that God will keep reminding me that He knows who I am and is there to help me to move forward to make an impact for Him and to keep my eye on the goal he has set before me.

Lord, may I simply walk with You. Take my hand and guide me through every moment of every day! Amen

November 5
Encouraging Us To Be Who We Are
By Sheryl Pepple

But we are not of those who shrink back and are destroyed, but of those who believe and are saved.
Hebrews 10:39 NIV

I have a whole new way of keeping time these days. There is the life before my husband died and the time since he died. Can I dare say it? The *life* since Dave died.

At first, there was the fog. The utter shock of finding out he would not be coming home. From there, I transitioned into some type of daily existence. Doing the things that had to be done, but little else. Eventually, I started to breathe again. And one day I laughed. And more time went on. And eventually, I started living again.

It is so hard at first, but somehow we move forward. Sometimes, it feels like we have to take it moment by moment, then it becomes day by day, and eventually, month by month. As I struggled to move forward in the beginning, I can remember desperately telling people - *I just need encouragement, I need to hear I am doing well, even if I'm not.*

I am sure most of us can make a list rather quickly of things we would recommend not saying to someone who has lost their husband. We all have examples of things that were not helpful and sometimes things that were even hurtful. But what would we tell our family, friends, coworkers and others, *is* helpful to say?

As I was reading in Hebrews this week, this verse spoke so deeply to my heart. We, my dear sisters, are not those *who shrink back and are destroyed*. It may feel like it for a little while. It may knock the breath out of us for a little while. But we go on. Eventually we start to actually *live* again. Because we are *those who believe and are saved*. We belong to Him and we have hope.

Most people have never been through the trial

and the pain of losing a husband. They can't relate and they don't know what to say. As one of my very wise friends, who walked through this journey with me said, "You are right, they can't relate, and you wouldn't want them to. We wouldn't wish this kind of pain on our worst enemy." I am so grateful for her wisdom, because if anyone said something that irritated me, I was able to be thankful they didn't understand.

But now we have the opportunity, and I believe the responsibility, to care for those who follow behind us. We have the opportunity to encourage them in this oh so difficult journey. How will I encourage them? By reminding them who we are - *not those who shrink back and are destroyed* and whose we are - *those who believe* and *are saved*.

I think these words speak so deeply to my heart because when my husband died, I felt like the whole world had been yanked out from under my feet. I struggled with who I was, I was no longer a wife, and what my purpose was, what do I do now.

The truth in this verse keeps us oriented on who we are and what our purpose in life is. When we are His, we are to persevere in our faith and to glorify Him. We have the chance for others to see God's love, His mercy and His faithfulness in our lives. We glorify Him simply by being, living with Him, step by step, day by day. No circumstance, no loss, can ever change or diminish His presence in our lives.

I cannot begin to imagine how difficult this journey would be without truly knowing God as Lord of my life. I am grateful that I know that Jesus died for my sins and because I believe in Him, I have eternal life. My hope is secure in Him. Oh, how I have needed Him. If you are struggling in your faith or if you have not come to that point where you know that you are His, please let us know so we can encourage you.

Dear Heavenly Father, I am so grateful that I am yours! I pray for comfort and encouragement through Your truth. Protect me from hopelessness. Help me be Your hands and feet in loving others and caring for them so that they may come to know You personally. In Your Son's Holy and Precious Name, Amen.

November 6
Thank You, Jesus, For Friendships That Make Us Feel Normal
By Kit Hinkle

Take your pay and go.
I want to give the one who was hired last
the same as I gave you.
Don't I have the right to do what I want with my own money?
Or are you envious because I am generous?'
Matthew 20:14-15 NIV

In this upcoming season of Thanksgiving, I am reminded how being thankful helps **us**. That was the topic of the message in church today – be thankful no matter what your situation is. Isn't that difficult to do when you have lost something so special to you?

As I looked around the sanctuary with so many loved ones around me and a pastor and kids would really love me, I had to let go of all that life hands me that's hard, and just be thankful.

I thought about the many women and men in my life who have stepped in at different seasons and repeatedly encouraged me to keep going, keep raising those kids, keep at the ministry, keep taking care of myself and working out, keep managing the finances, and keep reaching out to meet new people.

Thankful for friends who pick me up when it gets hard. They tell me I am doing great and how being a single mom doesn't make me odd--I am perfectly normal and God loves me.

Can I be that friend for you right now, sister? Can I tell you, seriously... you're doing great. God loves you, and you are not alone and you are very normal.

I want to leave you with this thought given to me by my pastor. In Matthew chapter twenty, a parable is told about a landowner who hires workers throughout the day, but pays them all the same generous pay at the end of the day. The workers who worked the whole day complained that those that only worked the last hour got the same pay.

Don't we do that? As I look at married couples I wonder, "Why do I have to raise my boys alone? Why do I have to handle attacks of the enemy by myself without a husband to hide behind?" I worked as hard, if not harder, at having a happy marriage as the next lady. But there she sits happily snuggled in her pew next to her man.

Where's my "Thankfulness Chair"?

The landowner replied to the complainers, he has the land. He has the right to be as generous as he wants to be with anyone.

I'm thankful for the blessings He gives me, and accept the hard parts more easily because I see the beauty in what He's doing through this season in my life. Thank You, Lord Jesus!

November 7
The God of Second Chances
By Nancy Howell

And the One who sat on the throne announced to His creation,
"See, I am making all things new. (turning to me)
Write what you hear and see, f
or these words are faithful and true."
Revelation 21:5 the Voice

God gives second chances. And third. And fourth, fifth, and sixth.

There's no limit to the "do-overs" our Lord grants each of His children.

Life is hard sometimes. Smooth-sailing days are not as frequent as any of us would wish.

The path we take, the journey we are on, it's not all rainbows, gumdrops, and sunshine.

Lucky for us, we have a God that never fails us. He's always just a whisper away.

He makes all things new.

All things....that includes your earthly

circumstances, whether you're facing heartache, emotional problems, monetary issues, a change in family dynamics, or faced with a life-changing loss.

He. Makes. All. Things. New.

And as far as I can tell, from reading His word, there's no expiration date on the renewing, no limit to the number of times we ask for a "do-over."

Unlike a car warranty, or insurance, or gym membership, His offer stands the test of time.

You can't buy it with money.

You can't barter for it.

You can't negotiate with Him to sweeten the deal.

It stands on its own.

Jesus paid the premiums already.

All you have to do is ask for the benefits.

Heavenly Father, thank You for the ultimate promise of making all things new. Again and again and again. I stumble, I fall, I get back up again. Help me remember that Your Word is always faithful and true, even when I am not. Amen.

November 8
A Feast
By Jill Byard

You prepare a table before me in the presence of my enemies
Psalm 23:5 NIV

Sometimes in the midst of my circumstances I

forget the real lasting power of the cross.

Like a solar eclipse, my troubles cast a dark shadow, blocking the hope of the cross. It's hard to see the light behind my circumstances. Events which were no fault of my own put me in unfriendly circumstances of confusion.

Staying here in the shadow is what the enemy is banking on. In his desperation for my heart, he tries to outshine the hope of the Son. He dances on broken hearts like they are the main attraction; just waiting on us to acknowledge his ability to eclipse the cross—his huge ego craving recognition.

When he starts this tap dance on my heart, I pull out the above verse. It gives me hope. I have read or heard it spoken about many times, but recently a Bible study speaker described the feast He prepares with such a powerful visual image that it remains stamped on my brain. I think about it daily. Our God, our Father, giver of all things, is preparing a feast for us right now.

A FEAST!

I am not talking about a drive-thru dinner you grab at Mickey D's. He's talking a catered affair dripping with every delicacy imaginable!

Think Fourth-of-July-celebration times infinity! And the clincher to the whole feast is that the enemy is going to have to sit and watch all of us enjoy all of God's plans.

No longer are our broken hearts the main attraction but the power of the promise that the cross offers; NEW LIFE!

In First Corinthians, Paul tells us how Christ wins over all this sting of death. In First Corinthians 15:57, he says victory will be through the Lord Jesus

Christ. Second Corinthians 4:18 describes the things that are unseen as eternal. Don't look at the seen—these we see here will fade away, and the unseen remains. Paul is talking about the sting of death. We all know the pain that the sting leaves for the family and friends who have been left behind. That sting, too, has the ability to cast shadows.

Oh, dear sisters in Christ, look what will come as a result of the real power of the cross—how Satan will be so thwarted. Our life on this earth is but a mist. When I feel the lies—"there is no end to my circumstances" and "my life has to be lived in the shadows", I will stop and remember that those shadows will never ever eclipse the power of the cross. He chose to give the gift of the cross for all our dark shadows. I'm going to choose to live in the glory of the cross each day.

Dear Father, help me walk in the glory of Your gift every day. Thank You for Your gift. I want to live in the power of all Your promises. Your life is more than just a story. It is hope for all my tomorrows. Amen

November 9
One Year Later
By Leah Stirewalt

It came. It went. The one year anniversary of my husband's suicide. I had been preparing for that day. I didn't know what to expect. How would I feel? Would it be a day of tears? Would I feel a sense of relief that I completed a year of "the firsts"?

Ahh...the firsts...

The first time I attended church without him

The first time I slept in our bed alone

My first wedding anniversary as a new widow

The first Thanksgiving

The first Easter

His first birthday in Heaven

The first Christmas

The first time I laid eyes on his gravestone after being placed in the ground

The first time I went to visit my in-laws, and he didn't accompany me

My first birthday as a widow

The first Valentine's Day

And...of course...the first anniversary of his death

The list is endless. The "firsts" could go on and on it seems. I had a year full of them. And, I was somewhat disappointed to learn that "the seconds" are often worse than the firsts. Seriously? That's not what I expected to hear, but I'm trying to be wisely prepared emotionally, or as much as I reasonably can be.

For me, part of that attempt at wise preparation has been tackling my grief experience head-on. I haven't hidden my grief (okay – maybe parts of it – the parts that need to be strictly between God and me).

On the contrary, I've tackled it quite openly through any tool I can get my hands on. Prayer, God's Word, books, people, other widows, counseling, GriefShare, blogging, and journaling have been many of the resources that I've employed to aid me through this first year as a suicide widow. I shudder to think the place that I would be emotionally if I had chosen to just sit down, curl up in a ball, and do nothing! That's not what my husband would want me to do, and it's certainly not where God wants to find me.

However, the enemy would love to find me there. The deceiver himself would want nothing more than to see me give up on life. If I give up, I'm ineffective for Kingdom work. That's right were Satan wants me. But God…

God has better plans for me…

Plans to prosper me and not harm me (Jeremiah 29:11)

Plans to give me a hope and a future (Jeremiah 29:11)

Plans to rescue me from the mire and not let me sink (Psalm 69:14)

Plans to deliver me from the deep waters (Psalm 69:14)

Plans to protect me with His love and truth (Psalm 40:11)

Plans to guide me and restore comfort to me (Isaiah 57:18)

Plans to make me strong, firm, and steadfast following suffering (1 Peter 5:10)

Friends…I choose to cling to God's plans for me. I choose NOT to believe the lies of the father of lies. God has never failed me and survival <u>with</u> healing during year one of widowhood has been one of his greatest areas to showcase his timeless faithfulness, grace, and love!

Continue to cling to His truth! Even on the hardest days…even with sobs pouring down your

face…cling   to   Him.   Speak   His
name…Jesus…Jesus…Jesus…at the name of Jesus,
the enemy must flee!

November 10
The Backlash of Another First
By Nancy Howell

I was doing great. Finished with a year's worth
of grief counseling, I "graduated," with my counselor
telling me to call only if I needed to talk. My boys?
Doing really well. The first nine weeks of school is
practically under their belts, and they have all A's.
They are thriving. We are living. We have established
a new normal.

Then why did I feel like I lost my husband all
over again last week? The raw pain, the emotions that
I thought I was past, came bursting through with a
vengeance I haven't felt in over a year—all because of
a stupid stomach bug. The scab that I hoped was well
on its way to becoming just a big old scar? It got
ripped off, and the blood trickled from it, fresh and
bitter.

All the "firsts" I thought I had experienced. I
had done the time. I have navigated wedding
anniversaries, his birthday, our sons' birthdays,
Thanksgiving, Christmas, New Year's, Valentine's
Day, my birthday, and every other special day I could
dream up. So imagine my dismay and surprise to find
that the one "first" I hadn't experienced without my

sweet husband was the first time I was sick without him.

Not just sick. So sick I could barely raise my head off of my pillow. So sick that it took every bit of strength I could muster to crawl out of bed and go to the bathroom, where I spent an inordinate amount of time. My boys were scared. Here was their strong mom, who had promised them she would always be there for them, curled up into a fetal position, head feeling like it was going to explode. I assured them it was "only" a virus, in a couple of days I would be fine.

Thankfully a dear friend took my sons to school since I was out of commission. I had a whole day to get through, alone.

As I lay there, head hurting, stomach churning, the day dragging, all I could think of was Mark. "If" he were still here, he would have taken the day off to take care of me. He would have taken boys to school. He would have brought a cool compress for my aching head. He would have made everything okay.

Instead, it was just me. Missing the physical presence of my dear husband. Lying in that bed, I grieved all over again. It was a terrible "first," being sick without him. I cried big old crocodile tears. I prayed. I wished for what could have been, again. I wondered how in the world I had been doing as well as I had.

This strong mama—able to shoot a shotgun, drill holes in masonry, write outdoor columns—who has jokingly commented, "I am woman, hear me roar…" was reduced to a puddle of tears, off and on, for seventy-two hours.

The length of the illness seemed to be directly proportional to the length of my pity party, my sad ode to me. After a long wallow of helplessness, feeling sorry for myself, I began to pray. First I prayed for healing from the virus. Then I prayed for healing for the ten year old, who unfortunately joined me in the big king-sized bed, twenty-four hours after my initial symptoms began. I prayed the nine year old would be immune from it (and he was). I prayed for God's presence to be enough, even without the physical presence of the man I loved for a quarter of a century.

As my younger son navigated preparing dinner for himself while two of us were in bed, unable to even think about food, I gave a prayer of thanksgiving. Thankful that I had equipped the boys for simple tasks, such as preparing a delectable peanut butter sandwich and a glass of milk. Thankful that I was beginning to feel better. Thankful for a cozy home, for two sons that love me, sick or well.

And as I slowly began to heal, the doubts of whether I was enough, whether I was up to this challenge of being a single mom dissipated and dwindled.

"Good friend, take to heart what I'm telling you; collect my counsels and guard them with your life.

Tune your ears to the world of Wisdom; set your heart on a life of Understanding.

That's right—if you make Insight your priority, and won't take no for an answer,

Searching for it like a prospector panning for gold, like an adventurer on a treasure hunt,

Believe me, before you know it Fear-of-God will be yours; you'll have come upon the Knowledge of God.

And here's why: God gives out Wisdom free, is plainspoken in Knowledge and Understanding.

He's a rich mine of Common Sense for those who live well, a personal bodyguard to the candid and sincere.

He keeps his eye on all who live honestly; and pays special attention to his loyally committed ones."

Proverbs 2:1-8 (the Message)

I claim the promise of wisdom, understanding, and knowledge. I am and will be enough for my family—as long as I have God. Amen.

November 11
The Here and Now
By Kit Hinkle

Until losing Tom, I never thought about how often loss shows up in so many art forms - movies, books, poetry, music. Now that I notice it, I often pick up clues on whether the artist knows first-hand how loss really feels. I know it by whether the work resonates with my experience.

Recently I watched a movie, which echoed in my heart for days after I saw it. The star of the sci-fi thriller played an agent who could merge his dreams into other people's dreams and steal ideas and thoughts. He had been doing it for years, but lately, since losing his wife, his love for her interfered. Memories of her kept entering into his dreams, sabotaging his missions. While he knew they were only memories, he indulged in them because it was all he had with her, and he could not bear to let her go. Finally he came to a point where he must let go. The scene was so touching, if you have been there and know what it's like to relish every thought and moment with your husband.

My husband entered my dreams constantly that year after he died, sometimes just to give me a refreshing smile for a moment until I realized he wasn't here to stay. Sometimes his visits would give me a message, although we know from Scripture that it was not really Tom but my mind processing thoughts of him.

In one dream he sat at a desk in the kitchen doing paperwork. I chatted with him, telling him how grateful I was that he was alive. He looked sad, and I could read his thoughts: "Alive, but what kind of life is this?" His mind said. I then remembered how the emergency room doctors tried to revive him for forty-five minutes after his heart stopped. I remembered standing by, waiting to hear whether they could revive him or not, wondering to myself, what kind of brain damage does a person who had little or no blood flow to the head have after that much time? I remembered thinking Tom is an active person—pushes his body to the limit. I then looked at him sitting at the desk and realized how limited his life would have been after serious injury to his heart and brain.

He still enters my dreams. When I decided to try dating, I dreamed Tom was alive. I was so embarrassed—how could I have gotten confused about Tom being dead or alive? Loyalty and fidelity mean everything to me. Tom then gave me that broad smile of his, and I felt his approval just before waking.

Back to the movie, in the final dream of his wife, the main character let his wife go because he realized that his mind could not completely imagine her through dreams. You need to see the movie to understand the intense emotion at which he forces himself to let go. His words, hinting at the struggle, went something like this: "I wish (you were here). I wish more than anything, but I can't imagine you with all your complexity, all your perfection, all your imperfection. You're just a shade of my real wife. You're the best that (my mind) can do, but I'm sorry, you're just not (the real thing)."

In the moment of watching that scene, I thought about the snippets of scenes of my life with Tom– those tracts which my mind played over and over for years: the day before he died when we teased and laughed together. The laughter in his eyes when he wrestled with the boys—the shy whisper in his voice when he admitted he might be saved—his indignation over a friend's husband when he walked out on her—the way he carried a piano into the house with no help at all—the way he'd hold a little baby as though there was nothing more natural in the world than for someone as boisterous and animated as he to be seen with a tender sprout of a child.

My teenage sons sat next to me that night when I watched the movie. I wondered if my sons had thoughts of loss about Dad. I wondered if they had any clue how the scene touched me. I decided it was well to let their thoughts about the scene be their own, and let our time watching the movie together be our time.

Memories are sweet, but my time with the boys was the here and now—it's what life's about.

November 12
The Journey Matters
By Teri Cox

For the Lord gives wisdom;
from his mouth come knowledge and understanding;
he stores up sound wisdom for the upright;
he is a shield to those who walk in integrity.

Proverbs 2:6-7 ESV

My thirteenth wedding anniversary was right around the corner. I wanted a perfect ending; now, I've learned the hard way, that **some songs don't rhyme and some stories don't have a clear beginning, middle or end**. Then again, some stories have endings that shatter previous scenes into a million pieces.

Life is about moving, not knowing. It's about adapting and changing. It's about taking a single moment and making the best of it; right then-no matter what happens next. When it's over, it's over-the moment is gone. No more second chances or wishes or dreams or could have beens; it's gone. So, take the single moments you are given and live them, RIGHT. Sometimes they will be beautiful, sometimes they will be painful but MOST of the time, they will be both; because, **pain and passion are kin**.

Don't regret something that once made you smile and brought you joy. Everything in life changes you in some way. If you don't accept the changes you don't accept yourself. Accept you; love you; live the best you you can be today. Be greater, be wiser, be more than you were yesterday. If you avoid the change, you lose the path and **the journey matters**.

So, what is your journey? Is it a journey that takes you a thousand miles away or to your "back yard"? Is it a journey that opens up new worlds or takes you to ones that repair what only your hands can make? Does it involve a million lives or just a select few?

No matter the path, the journey matters!

No matter the plan-because we plan and then life happens-the journey matters.

No matter the profit, the journey matters.

No matter the cost-Your journey matters!

So heal and move, Sisters. Don't stay stuck or buried under your grief blanket. Rise up and walk the path that God has made for you and only you. People are watching you and also watching God through you. The journey matters.

God, Help me remember You still adore me, I am loved and chosen by You. Help me see the path You have for me. The way I walk it matters because I may be the only Jesus the world ever sees. Help me on the journey You created for me. Amen.

November 13
The Wound
By Sarah Rodriguez

The other day I noticed a small wound on my

son's leg. It was turning the shade of red that looks like it's on the verge of getting infected. I gently held his leg down and started to pick at the wound to clean it out. He did not like it.

Actually, that might be an understatement. He was quite upset his Mama was picking on the ouchie on his leg. Boy, did he let me know it! He started to cry loudly, big fat tears running down his cheeks. I picked him up, gave him his favorite blanket, and rocked him calmly until he settled down. He's still so little he doesn't quite understand that in order for a wound to heal you have to take special care of it. That's what I wanted for my child.

Healing.

Complete healing.

But, in order to heal, you have to dig out the things that don't belong, then you must clean it out and bind it up. It's not a fun process to do so. It's painful and it hurts. But **we can never fully heal until we tend to our wounds the correct way**.

Sure, you could just put a band-aide on it, but that doesn't really correct the issue. It hides the wound and masks the pain for another day; when it manifests in unpredictable ways. It doesn't address the root of the issue, which is the wound itself.

I have found this to be the case in my grief. There are things I've had to do that literally feel like I'm picking at an open wound. They're the things that hurt but they are absolutely necessary for me to push through the pain to obtain the healing.

It can be something as big as knowing when to take his clothes out of the closet. It can be something as small as going to the grocery store alone when you used to go together. None of it is easy. All of it hurts. But in doing so, you're tending to your wound.

You're doing the things that are painful but give you strength and ensure healing for your soul.

Sure, it would be much easier to put a "band-aide" on the wound and save the cleansing for another day. It's not easy to tackle the things that cause you pain. It's not easy to live life without the one you love.

But what Gods wants, more than anything, is to heal your wound.

Yes, there will always, always, be a scar that remains, but it can become a scar that's healed properly. And when others see your scar you can boldly tell them about a wound that was so deep and so vast. Yet, a loving God swooped in and healed you from the inside out. It's what He longs to do.

The very next day I checked my son's leg. The wound, once so large, had shrunk to half the size. The bright red had long faded to his normal skin color. Gone with it was the wincing sting of pain he had displayed any time my hand was near it. The process wasn't fun for him to walk through. There were many things he didn't understand regarding the "whys" of the pain he had to endure.

But the end result was just as I had planned. The wound subsided and my boy healed and whole. Just what our God longs for you. If you'll only let Him.

Dear Jesus: I thank you that you long to heal every part of me that is wounded. I give You every part of me and surrender the healing process to You. I know that only You can make me whole again. Amen

November 14
Building Our Own Pillars of Remembrance
By Liz Anne Wright

> *In the future, when your children ask you,*
> *'What do these stones mean?'*
> *tell them that the flow of the Jordan was cut off*
> *before the ark of the covenant of the LORD.*
> *When it crossed the Jordan,*
> *the waters of the Jordan were cut off.*
> *These stones are to be a memorial to the people of Israel forever.*
> *Joshua 4:6b-7 NIV*

This past summer, my sons and I had the joy of going on a missions trip together. It was a wonderful week full of work, fun, growth, and new friends.

It also meant a lot of opportunity to share my testimony, both with our fellow workers and with others we met and ministered to. A lot of that naturally relates to what God has done in us and through us since Keith's death.

It used to be harder for me to share that testimony. It is, after all, very personal…and very painful. Sometimes I don't want to be reminded of what I have **lost**.

But recounting the events also helps me remember what I have **gained**.

I have **grown** through my trials. I have

learned to trust God more fully and completely as I look to Him now as, not just my Daddy, but my Husband as well.

And for that I am very **grateful**.

Dear sisters, if you have not shared your testimony, I encourage you to do so! It may not be easy at first. You may not be a naturally gifted speaker or writer. You may cry your way through it.

But, just like the pillar of stones Joshua had the Israelites set up when they crossed the Jordan, it will be there to remind people…even you…about the work God **has** done and **is** doing in your life. And that will be a blessing.

One of my new friends this week put it this way: "Everyone has their things that they have been through. But hearing how each of us goes through our trials **strengthens all of us**. Thanks for sharing."

I pray that you will boldly speak of what God has done and is doing for you and through you in this season. And that, because of your willingness to share, you reap the blessings of touching hearts for the God who has taken such good care of us.

Dear Father, help me speak boldly, even in this season of grief, of Who You are and what You have done. Help me to put up pillars of remembrance in my own heart to look to on the toughest days. Help me share with others when asked to, for the benefit of Your kingdom. In Jesus' precious Name, Amen.

November 15

Unfortunately Flawed or Wonderfully Made?
By Katie Oldham

When the questions come fast and furious and I see her wheels spinning, I know we're in for a fretful evening. She's not unlike most of us when worry sets in and we're sent into a frenzy; except she's six.

Somehow my sweet six year old possesses the mind of someone much older. Her kindergarten teacher emailed me earlier in the year to tell me she, *unfortunately*, has a mind much too mature for her age. Others express awe at her insatiable curiosity and desire for understanding.

She uses adult vocabulary in the correct context, often views situations from other's perspectives and analyzes possible outcomes for scenarios most six year olds overlook. I describe her as perceptive, persistent and often under-stimulated.

Sometimes, though, I wish she were different.

I feel frustrated at my inability to steer, stimulate or distract her. I fear her mind deters her from living life as a child, running whichever way the wind carries her!

Her teacher said the word that set the scene: *unfortunately*.

Then I look at my own life and see myself in her! She's a daughter after my own heart.

Perhaps, this too, is unfortunate. I wish I were different; less analytical, less structured, more fun and more fly-by-the-seat-of-my-pants.

We all look at ourselves and see ways we wish were different, don't we? We see the unfortunate, incompleteness in us. We want **more** out of ourselves, disappointed when we rarely reach the bottom of those lingering lists of to-dos. Then again, we'd like **less** of other things like impatience, procrastination or straining so hard towards some worldly sense of success.

We strive to live more like that other mom, that neighbor lady, that always put-together-women sitting at church in the pew in front of us. We want different of ourselves.

Then, His Word whispers…

I praise you because I am fearfully and wonderfully made;

your works are wonderful, I know that full well.

Psalm 139:14 NIV

Wonderfully made?! I think again of my daughter…and of myself…God created us in His likeness. He requires no reaching or striving for us to be anyone other than who He made us to be. In my focus on the 'unfortunate', I missed the part where I'm to praise Him that we are *'wonderfully made'*!

God gave me my darling daughter, wonderfully made, perfectly crafted for me to mother, different than any other daughter. She's not unfortunate or insatiable. She's simply sweet and filled with sincerity. She longs to learn and motivates me to seek ways to stimulate her.

I watched her with worry rather than recognizing the wonder in her. I wanted to squelch her spinning wheels instead of seeing her beautiful uniqueness! Sure, like any child (or adult, for that matter), she requires redirection and discipline, but she need NOT be anything other than who God made her.

Through this shift in my parenting perspective

I can see myself in a different light. I'm alright. In fact, I'm wonderfully made, too! It's okay that I'm not the funny one in the bunch because I offer a listening ear. Instead of feeling bound by my innate need for organization, I've found ways to see structure as a strength.

We must make peace with who we are so that we are not constantly distracted from our purpose by our own insecurities. **Have you, dear sisters, made peace with who you are and found purpose in how GOD crafted you?**

The most beautiful YOU is the one God made you to be. He sees you through eyes of love! Can you too, view yourself lovingly as a complete creation in Him? What quality about yourself can you embrace and use for your Creator?

Yes, YOU can be used for God's GOOD just the way you are!

When you start self-judging or wishing you were more like someone else, remember the Lord labored over YOU. He put you here for His purpose and wants you to live out YOUR life, unlike anyone else's.

God's given us unique personalities, purposes and imperfections. You can use every ounce of yourself for His greater good, even your imperfections.

Deuteronomy 10:12 says: '....fear the Lord your God, to walk in obedience to him, to love him, to serve the Lord your God with all your heart and with all your soul.' NIV

Serve Him with all your heart and all your soul, not just the parts of yourself you

approve of.

Instead of seeing yourself as unfortunately flawed (as I was seeing my daughter and myself), shift your perspective to a more Biblical one and see yourself as COMPLETE in and through Him.

Dear Father, Master Creator, I pray I won't judge myself too harshly. Instead of seeing myself through earthy eyes, I am undistracted by self-expectation and striving to be someone different than You made me to be. I praise You for the creativity and completeness You put in each one of us and ask that You show me how to use my unique qualities for Your glory! Amen

November 16
How Do You Hold Thoughts Captive?
By Kit Hinkle

> *We destroy arguments and every lofty opinion*
> *raised against the knowledge of God,*
> *and take every thought captive to obey Christ.*
> *2 Corinthians 10:5 ESV*

We all have those days--when you are trying to give it your all. You know you're blessed. Yes, you've lost your best friend, but God has blessed you in so many ways. Maybe with your children. Maybe with friends. Maybe He's provided for you, or given you options for a new life.

Maybe it's simply the peace of knowing He is in control and that your salvation is safe with Him. Be sure that's there, because knowing He died for you helps you remember that this grief is only but a moment in the short time we have on this earth, and the reality is the everlasting joy He will give us in eternity!

Here's a tip my boy gave me--place a bracelet on one arm. Every time wrong thinking creeps in your head, stop what you are doing and move the bracelet to the other arm, meanwhile shifting your thoughts to God's thoughts--remembering His purpose for you, the work He has for you, the goodness in your life, and your thankfulness.

When you start to think, "wow--I lost so much when I lost my husband," try to remember the Gospel. It's all about surrender. In order to have salvation and everlasting life, there is only one requirement--that we die to all we think we're entitled to here. We surrender it all the Christ, Who Himself surrendered all to the cross for our sake.

If you think you've lost, think for a moment all what Christ lost. His friends, his supporters, His popularity, His comfort--to the point of suffering a more grueling torture than any of us can imagine. And then finally, His life.

And as you move that bracelet, shift your thoughts from what you have lost, to what He gave up, to finally what He gave you in exchange-- salvation, new life--including a new life here with purpose!

Meanwhile, to fulfill His purpose, we need to bend our minds to obey God's thoughts not the enemy's.

My older son took the bracelet a step further. "Mom," he said, "Try putting the bracelet on your ankle-- that will really make you stop and rethink your thinking!"

Ha Ha! Now there's a thought!

What works for you, sisters?

Hey, God. Can You give me some techniques for how to actually take Your suggestion to hold every thought captive? Amen.

November 17
No Tear Wasted
By Leah Stirewalt

"The Lord will not waste a single tear that you've shed since Chris died. Not one." If she's said it to me once, she's said it at least a dozen times. My friend has been quick to reassure me the tragedy of my husband's death would not be wasted…that God would be glorified, even through something so horrific as suicide and He would use me in spite of my brokenness.

In the early days and months, those were tough words to swallow. I believed her, but I simply couldn't see it. My "new normal" life as a widow seemed so dysfunctional.

I couldn't make simple decisions.

I couldn't get through most days without an emotional breakdown.

The simplest things in life became the most difficult.

How in the world would God use this "mess"

of a woman for His glory? While I didn't know or understand just then, I still committed myself to Him and whatever work He planned to do through me.

Suicide is such an ugly word – or at least it seemed that way to me at the time. Anytime someone would ask how my husband passed away, I would honestly share, "he committed suicide". You could almost visibly see the shift in expression or movement that resulted in a little more space between us. It made people uncomfortable. They didn't know what to say or how to respond. And you know what? I totally understood that. I really did.

Prior to Chris' suicidal death, I wouldn't have known how to respond either…I would have wanted to withdraw that question as soon as it escaped my lips if I had known that would be the answer. However, God has definitely made me sympathetic and empathetic to those that are "suicide survivors" – the term officially used for family members left to survive the suicide of a loved one. As a result of having "survived" this experience myself, I've been acquainted with numerous other women (especially) and a few men and children that have lost relatives to suicide. I've been privileged to pray for them/with them, to pass along resources that have helped me along my journey. I've been asked a couple of times to share "my story" of God's redemptive hope that's been poured out upon me through this heartbreak. I've been asked to guest blog about my journey upon occasion and to even "counsel" with other suicide survivors.

Each time my throat wells up and my eyes form new tears (because, that continues to happen ladies…even after healing), I praise God that He's not allowing one of those tears to be wasted. While I wish I never had to experience something so horrific, I am so thankful that God has allowed my tragedy to be used for His glory!

Has it been easy? Far from it! But, God doesn't ask us to do "easy" – just to trust Him and give Him our "difficulties". I had no other choice ladies…I couldn't carry this burden alone. I had to give it to Him. All of it. And in return? He's restored so much more than I could ever imagine!

*The Lord is my shepherd, I shall not be in want. He makes me lie down in green pastures, he leads me beside quiet waters, he **restores** (emphasis mine) my soul. He guides me in paths of righteousness for his name's sake.*

Psalm 23:1-3 NIV

<u>November 18</u>
Co-Incidence or God-Incidence?
By Karen Emberlin

But watch out!
Be very careful never to forget
what you have seen God doing for you.
May his miracles have a deep and permanent
effect upon your lives!
Tell your children and your grandchildren
about the glorious miracles he did.
Deuteronomy 4:9 TLB

Have you ever had a set of circumstances in

your life that were so unexpected and so complex that you knew there was no other way it could have happened except by divine appointment?

Some people refer to inexplicable, uncanny, timely, and/or especially appropriate happenings as coincidences. But I like to think of them as "God-incidences" – blessings and miracles from God that have and are making a permanent effect on my life.

After my husband's sudden and unexpected death, I had the full responsibility of managing my health issues. I have been a diabetic for fifty-nine years and for forty-eight years, my husband Don was very instrumental in helping me monitor my sugar and insulin levels on a daily basis. He was always there to make sure I did not go too low at night and took care of me when it did.

It was a scary feeling not to be able to "confirm" with him that I was making the right choices and the thought of living alone was not something I even wanted to think about. I was able to stay with my daughter and her family for several months after my husband's death until I could determine what was best as a long term solution.

During that time of transition my step-dad passed away and my Mom was alone again. I had never thought about returning to the place I grew up, but things began to fall in place and, before I knew it, I was planning a move back to my home town to live with my Mom in a new apartment in a wonderful retirement facility. I did not have to live alone and medical "help" would be available if I needed it!

A couple of months after my move, I began to search for doctors to help with my diabetes and some complications I have from it. It was soon determined I really needed to consider an insulin pump to help get my diabetes under better control. I needed to find an endocrinologist. I really wanted to go back to my "old" doctor who treated me before I moved some twenty years ago. I was told he was near retirement and not taking any new patients. I finally got an appointment with a doctor, but had many reservations.

A few weeks before my appointment, I went on a trip with the "seniors" from our church. There were seven of us on the trip who were widows and I knew all but one of them. As we began to spend time together, I realized this one lady I did not know well, not only shared the journey of widowhood with me, but she was a diabetic, on an insulin pump, a nurse, went to my "old" doctor, and only lived five minutes from me.

After a few conversations with her and a phone call to my "old" doctor's office, I had an appointment to see him within a few weeks! It was such a blessing to return to my doctor as he knew the struggles I have with the diabetes. My new "purple" pump was ordered and I was scheduled for training to begin using it on January second.

I was a bit concerned about that date, as it was the second anniversary of my husband's death, but I was confident that I could handle it, knowing that getting started on the pump was important. January second turned out to be a very icy, snowy, and cold morning.

It was decided it was not safe to travel to the place I was to meet with the people to get this process started. The trainers, who were to meet with me, are from the pump manufacturer and only come to our area once a month. New training was scheduled for February sixth. I was disappointed since I was very "ready" to get this going but had to accept it.

The next day I received a phone call from my doctor telling me she knew I needed to start the pump before February and had received authorization from the manufacturer to train me herself. She asked me to meet her on January fourth - a Saturday!

My friend drove me to meet with the doctor and was there so she could understand all the settings. My "new" friend and I not only share the journey of widowhood, but understand the demands of controlling diabetes!

I truly believe all of these events were not mere coincidences, they were orchestrated by God, just as He has many others in the past. But why should I be surprised? God knows me personally (Psalm 139) – He knew that my husband's time to help me was over, so He placed another one of His children in the right place at the right time to help and be a blessing to me!

Heavenly Father, I know that there is no such thing as co-incidences in my life. Help me to watch and listen for the God-incidences that occur every day of my life. Thank You for the many I have experienced in the past. Help me to share with others how You are working in my life – may it be an encouragement and blessing to someone. Amen

November 19

Rediscovering Whose We Are
By Sheryl Pepple

See, I have engraved you on the palms of my hands;
your walls are ever before me.
Isaiah 49:16 NIV

In just an instant we transition from being a wife to being a widow…Not only do we feel like our whole world is changed, we also feel like we don't know who we are anymore. I was a wife, a helpmate, a best friend, a lover, a business partner, a traveling companion, a co-parent, and so many other roles. Now I am alone. I am no longer a wife; I no longer have those roles. If I dwell on what was, I get overwhelmed with sadness and filled with anxiety. What now? Who am I?

The key to our peace is remembering *whose* we are…

As I continue to walk through this journey, I am amazed at the sheer magnitude of the pain…and at the same time continually humbled by God's tenderness and love that carries me through the pain. His Word tells us that He will never leave us nor forsake us, but nothing is more reassuring than when we see or feel His presence in our lives.

I struggle with truly accepting that He loves me --- deeply, personally and always. I struggle with the temptation of thinking somehow I can "earn" His love by being good. His Word tells me differently, but still my heart struggles to accept His love, His truth.

Today, I would like to share a personal example of how He showed me His presence and His love in a way that has forever changed my perception of who I am to Him.

I was going through some difficult days a few months after my husband's death, and my attitude was definitely not pleasing to Him or anyone else around me. And trust me - that's putting it mildly. I was actually leading a Bible study group one evening during that time, when the teacher on the study DVD made the point that God speaks to us every day through our daily reading of His word. With my not-so-wonderful-attitude I started arguing with God (in my head, fortunately, not out loud!), *Well that's not true, because I read Your Word today and You had nothing for me. Where are You when I need You so desperately?* I had been reading in Exodus and the description of the tabernacle and I wasn't hearing anything, just a whole lot of details about His dwelling place. Blah, Blah, Blah. (I warned you, my attitude was not good.)

The next day, while sitting at my desk, I received an email devotional that talked about the importance of names. That made me start thinking about my new grandson's name and its meaning. I went on the internet to start some research on names. And from there I started wondering what my name meant. Fifty years old and I had no idea what my name meant. Over the years, I wished many times that I had a nice Biblical name like Grace or Sarah. But nope, my name is Sheryl, and I even have to deal with a name that everyone wants to spell with a C. Nothing special about me or my name. Little did I know that God had prepared this moment for me to discover how truly special I am to Him through my very special name.

In my research I quickly discovered that my name is derived from two words, the first a French word "Cherie" which means cherished or beloved and the second part of my name is derived from Beryl, a precious gemstone found in the foundation of the tabernacle. Funny, that was what I had been reading about the day before when I was reading in Exodus. God had been speaking to me, I just missed it.

A few days later I was reading in Revelation and there it was again, Beryl the gemstone in the foundation of the city walls in Heaven. And slowly but surely it started to seep into my heart in a whole new way, how truly precious I am to Him. I am His beloved; I am a gemstone in the foundation of the city walls of Heaven. His timing was perfect; He saved that gift for me until I was fifty, a recent widow, and just when I needed Him most. My dear sisters, I don't know exactly in what way He will show you during this journey how much He loves you but I know He will. And His timing will be perfect, just when you need it most. Just like our verse, our names are engraved on His palms, our walls are before Him. We are precious, we are loved, and we are His. Our peace comes from knowing not who we are but by knowing *whose* we are…

Dear Heavenly Father, thank You for loving me more than I can possibly comprehend. My heart is broken, I am weary, but I am loved and I am Yours! Father, please let me feel Your presence in my life today, and let this truth (that I am so loved that my name is engraved on the palms of Your hands) seep into my heart in a new and deeper way. In Your Son's precious and holy name, Amen.

November 20
In God's Time
By Nancy Howell

Yet God has made everything beautiful
for its own time.
He has planted eternity in the human heart,
but even so,
people cannot see the whole scope of God's work
from beginning to end.

Ecclesiastes 3:11 NLT

I remember reading this verse shortly after becoming a widow. Snuggled up in my big bed, between two little boys, ages eight and nine, as they drifted off to sleep.

Hot tears coursed down my cheeks, creating pools of salty bitterness as I soaked in these Old Testament words.

Beautiful?

How in the name of Jesus Christ could God EVER make something beautiful out of this dark, lonely, oppressive mess I found my family smack dab in the midst of?

I couldn't fathom how to get through the night, much less how to get through the emotions weighing on me so heavily. Sometimes I wondered if I could even take another breath, the pain was devastating.

Two boys no longer had their daddy physically by their sides. I no longer had my partner, the one person (this side of heaven) that loved me for me.

I felt like I was moving in slow motion, while the world around me moved at warp speed. Life continued, despite my best efforts to keep it at bay.

Primarily a New Testament girl until age forty-eight, I discovered the Old Testament offered me more during my grieving process.

Don't get me wrong, I love the New Testament and what it means for every born-again Christian. For the most part, it is an easy read. Salvation, the life of Jesus, the disciples' stories, the spreading of the Gospel to distant shores---it gives us our heavenly hope.

Whereas I consider the New Testament more of an answer to eternal life in general, the Old Testament, in my opinion, is the Bible's meat and potatoes.

Sometimes it's not pretty. Sometimes it's downright difficult to digest. But for folks in the midst of a crisis, where lollipops and rainbows and perfection don't exist, the Old Testament is the grit and soul of the Bible.

God's timing? I've never understood it.

And, at age fifty, I think I've finally become okay with that.

Reading the heart-wrenchingly beautiful book of Ecclesiastes from start to finish as a widow of three months was-difficult-but-necessary for this Texan.

"Yet God made everything beautiful for its own time..."

Really, God? Where's the beauty in watching my sons suffer?

Where's the beauty in being alone, after being part of a couple for over twenty years?

Where's the beauty in figuring out how to mow a yard, replace a light fixture, repair a clothes dryer?

Just how many buckets of tears can one woman cry?

The sad list changed constantly. It was seemingly endless. But God's answer remained the same: unchanging, unwavering, and steadfast.

The widow must trust God's timing.

I drank in that book of Ecclesiastes for the first time a bit over two years ago.

Looking back now, I can see the hand of God, the interweaving of beauty through the ashes and the pain of my family during this journey.

Life is different. That may be the understatement of the year for me.

I'm not who I was. Neither are my boys.

We bear the scars of losing a daddy and husband, a best friend and provider. But the scars are proof of our healing.

God has taken this very-bad-no-good-horrible-mess and transformed it into beauty.

In His time.

Laughter has replaced the tears in our home. We smile, sometimes until our cheeks hurt. We belly laugh until our sides hurt.

In His time

I run to upbeat contemporary Christian tunes, pounding the pavement, thanking God for the beauty He's created from the ashes of my life.

In His time.

Sisters, do not ever doubt the Word of God.

He will keep His promises.

Pour over Scripture, especially in the Old

Testament, to soothe your souls.

Don't compare your life, your circumstances, to anyone else's. Grief is different for everyone.

Whenever a widow friend told me shortly after my husband's death that one day I would just wake up, finding life was again worth living, I smiled sweetly, thanked her, all the while thinking, "Yeah, right..."

But right she was. One day a couple of months ago, I did wake up, like I had been in a deep slumber. I am once again eager to experience life, ready for whatever God has in His plans for my boys and me.

You will do the same, dear one.

In His time.

Heavenly Father, I give You thanks for my storm and for the beauty that will come from it. Help me be patient, to hold to Your promises of making everything beautiful in its own time. When I am in the midst of the bad, it's so difficult to look up. Thank You for Your patience, for Your persistence in my healing. I pray I may be renewed by these words, by the promise of healing and beauty. Your time must be my time. In the name of Your blessed Son I ask it all, Amen.

November 21
Singing the Second Year Blues
By Elizabeth Dyer

Even in laughter the heart may ache.
Proverbs 14:13 NIV

Crazy things I have done without pain-killers: I had a root canal once without anesthesia (because the dentist was a quack). I gave birth twice without an epidural (because I was afraid of needles).

Which brings me to grief…Grief in the second year seems like having surgery without anesthesia, because you now feel every emotion, raw and stinging.

When I joined the sisterhood of widowhood, I loved the encouragement and strength that these ladies at AWM/aNS gave me. But I have to admit, the comments they made, with a sly wink at the others, about the second year kind of unnerved me. They suggested I wouldn't have experienced the hardest year of my life during the first year of grief.

"I can't hear you, I can't hear you!" I plugged my ears and shouted to no one in particular.

I am now in the middle of year two. And I get it now…I understand what my sisters were saying. You know that fog that filled your brain during the first year of widowhood? It has been lifted and reality has settled in. The reality that all those jokes you shared with someone are left hanging in the air with no one there to finish the joke or smile as you say the movie or song line. The reality that you are single parenting and you are barely hanging on some days. The reality that the love you shared with that special person is over. The marriage is cut short. The fathering has ended.

Many of my widow sisters weighed in on this subject. One issue in the second year is that some of the people who wanted to help so much at the beginning are no-where to be found during the middle of year two. Another issue is that people (including us!) expect to be further along in grief so that it doesn't actually exist anymore.

Sometimes we think or feel we should be over this already and just move along. Haven't we cried enough? Haven't we seen enough school programs without dad that we can go without crying this time? Haven't we sat in our usual pew at church enough times that we don't cry as we sit there without our loved one?

No, we haven't. You are probably going to cry again and again. And that's okay.

I don't want my friends to worry that they can't say things about their married life because they are afraid I will be sad if I hear it. Sometimes they will say something that will trigger a memory for you about your husband.

You will have sad moments and that's okay.

One sister heard grief described this way:
Year   One: Grief   walks   over   you
Year   Two: Grief   walks   closely   beside   you
Year Three: You walk over grief

So year two is feeling the grief without the anesthesia. The emotions are felt more acutely. Reality becomes permanent.

Stay (or get back) into God's Word during the second year. Fill your mind with praise songs in order to keep your heart in tune with God's heart. Surround yourself with believers that speak truth into your life.

Which year are you in? Has the fog cleared and you are feeling every emotion now more than ever?

When you are in the grief of the first year, it is hard to imagine feeling grief deeper. But be aware that you might experience grief in a new and different way during your second year. Arm yourself with Scripture by reading the Psalms or by reading a book on the promises of God. Pray for another widow sister to walk with on the grief journey. Look for ways to get involved in ministry at your local church. Offer to babysit for a young mother weekly. Help in the toddler room during the VBS week at your church. Love on someone else. **It won't make the grief go away, but it will give you a purpose**. And we all need a purpose in life.

Father God, Thank You for Your love for me today. Draw me to Yourself when I struggle the most. Show me a purpose, a place where I can minister to someone else. Give me endurance on the grief journey. Thank You for walking along beside me. Amen

November 23
Waking Up to God
By Kit Hinkle

My stepson's favorite rock artist has lyrics to a song which describes the world around us as filled with people living in a comatose state—minds saturated with media and world messages that keep us from seeing the reality of God. The CD artwork shows a little boy standing with a spellbound look on his face and a giant plug, which he must have just pulled out from a wall. When you open the artwork, you see what he's looking at—a twisted discombobulation of electronics which must have been keeping him in a comatose state, until that moment.

"That moment" is what I wanted to talk to you about.

I had one of those moments! Like that boy who had just unplugged the media.

Last weekend I found a way to unplug my discombobulation (yes, that's a word!)—that twisted feeling I've had since losing my husband three years ago.

My pastor always told us how to do it, how to take that focus off of your own circumstances and get a new perspective.

It's service.

My teens and I joined a team of thirty people at my church to head to the Appalachian mountains to minister to families in a coal mining town.

To say we were blown away by what we witnessed in the hills of Appalachia is an understatement. We expected poverty and hearts eager for shoes. What we didn't expect was unimaginably severe circumstances, an absolute hardship for something so simple as shoes, and hearts starving for prayer and understanding—kids and parents eager to find the real Jesus Who can help them.

We returned home wanting to pray more. After seeing the need people had, our home, even without a husband or father, felt perfect because we had Father God in control! And I slept. So soundly, and not because I was exhausted. I slept that peace of knowing it's all going to work out, because it is. He's really in control.

I think of how many times I slip into a rut and look at what's wrong instead of what's right. If you find yourself falling into that pattern, I hope my message helps to open your eyes to how **serving others can help you**.

Of course, if you're new to your loss, please know that grief has tears and you need the time to heal. Our challenge is to know when the Lord is calling you to move beyond the tears and what to do to step out and move forward. **Serving others is one tools you can use to take your focus upward and away from your circumstances.**

If a mission trip is not feasible for you, try something smaller. My kids and I have served at a soup kitchen. I have taken teens whose families agree with the philosophy of making service a habit.

I can't tell you I always feel great when I leave to go to that soup kitchen. Some mornings when I'm already scheduled to go, I'm not feeling like going and I'm distracted with burdens of the day. I go anyway. When I get to the kitchen, I start my work—lifting canned foods in the pantry, handing out servings of a lunch, or peeling potatoes for a meal. Within minutes the movement of my joints synchronized to the sounds around me and the needs on the faces of those that I'm serving all work together to melt away my self- focus and re-energize me, returning me to my life with a new perspective. It's not hopeless—my life, I mean. It's not overwhelming. Really, I have it pretty well.

So do you.

November 24
Keeping Up Appearances
By Nancy Howell

"Hey, you look good!"

I wish I had a quarter for every time I've heard that in the past couple years. Well-meaning acquaintances, friends, former co-workers tell me this, and it's very sweet of them. My inner voice quickly puts me in my place, telling me, "Man, you must have really looked bad for a few months after becoming a widow!"

I do look better. My eyes are once again clear and sparkly. There's a spring in my step, and I am a woman with a purpose.

Well, several purposes--seems I don't have enough hours in the day, days in the week, to accomplish all that is on my plate.

Busy is good. Busy keeps me putting one foot in front of the other, and my "to-do" list is finally getting some items crossed off, some of which have been there for months.

But what about what I look like on the inside? Am I as put together as I seem on the surface?

One person knew me inside and out. He could look into my eyes and see through the fluff, the stylish exterior and the smile plastered on my face--- straight into my insides, into my soul. But he's no longer beside me. He's up in heaven now.

I so want my insides to match my outside!

Don't get me wrong. I have good stretches. I have days where I have the world on a string. God has been so good in the midst of all of this bad, and I am so grateful for all the blessings and opportunities that have come my family's way.

But many of them have come my direction because of my husband's death. If he were still alive:

I wouldn't be writing for this ministry.

I wouldn't be a weekly outdoors writer for the local newspaper.

I wouldn't be speaking in front of groups, sharing my story.

I wouldn't be writing a book.

I would still be teaching preschool, loving on two and three year old children. I would still be the devoted wife of my college sweetheart. I would be supporting him, keeping our house in order, helping him raise our two sons. His dreams and my dreams merged together, as they should in a good marriage, to become "our" dreams.

His death, though, changed all of that.

"Our" dreams had to be put on hold.

Some, I had to just let go of. That still hurts.

Others, I've adapted to fit our current circumstances and family dynamics.

A few new ones have come to light, too, as my sons and I begin to find new purpose and meaning in what we've been given.

Time is healing us, because we have proactively worked to heal.

And things are going okay. The good stretches seem to be getting longer and longer, although whenever I hit a bump in the road, I still feel the raw, sad grief that haunted me 24/7 for months.

I still cry. I still miss my husband. I think I always will.

Others who have been widowed for longer

periods of time tell me that it will get better. The pain will lessen, they insist, and life will become more normal.

At this place in my journey, I'm not so sure.

Because my insides don't match my outside.

Thankfully, God knows all of this, even before I bring it to Him in prayer. I'm sure He does His share of shaking His head at me, at my circumstances. For my insides to match my outside, I have to remember that He and He alone has the power to make them alike. And that's not going to happen as long as I'm sitting on the sidelines, hoping for change.

God wants me to be proactive in this. He expects me to do my part. And I've been most likely not holding up my end of the bargain. Hence, the insides are not as "pretty" as my exterior facade.

How do I get my interior to be as pretty and as put together as my exterior? I must "do the time"...reading God's Word, praying for guidance and healing, allowing Him to work out the details (both big and little) that drive me crazy. I haven't found any shortcuts, any "Cliff Notes" that will help.

This transformation is an on-going process. The more I put into it, the more I will get out of it.

The more I immerse myself in God's ways, in what He would have me do, following the map that He has given me, the more I feel put together on the inside.

And sisters, if there's hope for my sad, not-so-pretty interior, there is most certainly hope for yours.

Friends, when life gets really difficult,
don't jump to the conclusion that God isn't on the job.

*Instead, be glad that you are in the very thick of what Christ
experienced.
This is a spiritual refining process,
with glory just around the corner.
So if you find life difficult because you're doing what God said,
take it in stride. Trust him.
He knows what he's doing, and he'll keep on doing it.*
1 Peter 4:12,13, 19 The MSG

*Creator God, I ask for help on my insides. Oh how I want to
be whole again, both inside and out! I long for the day when my
sadness will be turned into gladness, when my interior self is as
put together and pretty as what I show to the outside world. I
don't want to forget the love I had for my late husband, but I
want to be able to move forward joyfully, and enjoy the life that
You have given to me. I want to honor what I had, but I know
I need to keep on living. You created me for a specific purpose.
Help me discover just exactly what that purpose is. In Jesus'
name I ask it all, Amen.*

November 25
Bittersweet
By Sherry Rickard

*So Moses brought Israel from the Red Sea...
and they went three days in the wilderness and found no water.
And when they came to Marah, they could not drink of the
waters of Marah for they were bitter...
And the people murmured against Moses, saying,
What shall we drink?*

And he [Moses] cried unto the Lord;
and the Lord showed him a tree,
which when he had cast into the water,
the waters were made sweet.
Exodus 15:22 -25 KJV

I remember leaning on this passage so heavily when my husband was ill. Every doctor visit was bad news and disappointment. At home, it was so painful to watch my husband suffer the effects of his illness and to be so helpless. My husband was unable to work for a time period due to his illness so our comfortable life became very uncomfortable...or should I say very quickly unaffordable. Every aspect of our once carefree life became hard and heavy.

My husband in his most quiet moments, when it was just the two of us and, even when I wandered into a room in which he was alone, was the definition of peace. He didn't rail at God and ask why. He wasn't mad at his diagnosis. He was the definition of peace and contented joy, even in our darkest hour.

He would often say that he had the golden ticket. If he was called Home, he got to start eternity in the presence of his Savior; and if his body was miraculously cured here on earth, he got to spend more time with us. He would always end with, "Either way, I'm a big winner!"

Me, on the other hand, I was a quiet "Marah" (bitter, like the waters Moses found). I knew that God would be glorified in whatever happened and that He would sustain me, but I was growing quietly bitter the longer our journey took. It wasn't something that was apparent, it was a quiet background noise to my everyday life.

Then on Valentine's Day, the Lord lovingly allowed me to realize that He was going to bring Bill Home. That was my most bitter moment of all. As I put my lips to my husband's lips in the ICU at Duke Hospital and we kissed for the last time this side of eternity, God gently loosened my grasp on my husband and took him Home. At that moment, my heart wasn't broken, it was ripped from my chest and there was complete emptiness in its place.

How could my heart heal when it had been removed from my body?

How could God ask this of me?

As each minute, hour, day, week, month, year, and now several years, passed...God sent me experiences; one by glorious one that were filled with sweetness. Slowly, the pain (that never completely goes away)was insulated by sweet memories to the point that I could bear the journey God asked me to take. I am to the point now that I can bear the pain because of the sweetness that surrounds it; if that makes sense. I laugh more days than I cry. I can remember fun times spent with my husband and not feel the heaviness of him not being here.

Just as in the Scripture above, the water was too bitter to drink and the Lord had to show Moses God's hand-crafted tree. Once it was dipped into the water, the water was made sweet, and the Israelites were able to drink it. In much the same way, God has taken my bitterness and He has dipped His beautiful hand into it. In doing so, He has made it turn to sweetness. And with this change, I am able to bear the journey. As hard as it is to believe, there have been many points on the journey that were very sweet.

Dear Lord, Help me remember that if Your hand is in it, it will be sweet. Help me remember to lean in and feel Your presence in everything. Help me surrender to You and allow Your love to sustain me. Thank You for turning the bitter and unbearable into bearable sweetness. In Your Precious Son's Name, Amen

November 26
Heart Specialist
By Erika Graham

The LORD your God is in your midst,
a mighty one who will save;
He will rejoice over you with gladness;
He will quiet you by His love;
He will exalt over you with loud singing.
Zephaniah 3:17 (ESV)

I got to hear my babies' heartbeats today!

And it brought me back…Back to eight years ago when they were tucked safely in my belly, that whirring sound during my many ultrasounds, telling me they were strong and healthy, that everything was right in the world.

Today was the day! I got to see and hear those beating hearts on the monitor just as I did so long ago. It hit hard, listening to that beautiful sound again.

Memories flooded my mind as I watched each of them climb up on the table...as I watched and listened to their strong hearts beat on the screen.

Memories of my husband and me crying childless tears...

Memories of the sweet sound of the heartbeat on the ultrasound when we finally became pregnant with our daughter...

Memories of struggles with infertility again.

Memories of the doubly sweet sound of **two** little heartbeats going strong inside me, when we became pregnant with twin boys.

I realized only my husband would love and appreciate that sound and all those memories as much as me.

Reality hit yet AGAIN!

My husband, my story keeper, my partner in all this life stuff, is not here.

I choked back tears as I tried to focus on this sweet specialist and all she was sharing with me about my boys' precious hearts.

But, my mind wandered. It wandered off into the place my "widow brain" takes me at any given moment; memories, regrets, sorrows, nostalgia, melancholy, jealousy, fear, loneliness...You name it, it's all there.

As I drove home from the appointment, getting the all clear (Praise God) nod from the cardiologist, I cried tears of relief and tears of sadness.

I felt a sense of relief because the trip to the heart specialist for my boys was complete. I could now release the worry I carried for the last few weeks, from the moment the pediatrician said she heard something and was sending them to a cardiologist, through to our appointment today.

I felt sadness because I had to do this all alone, that Scott missed this day.

And I really missed him!

I was grateful that I could cry out to my own cardiologist, my heart specialist:

Lord, I need you now. I miss Scott, today especially! I don't have the one person who was in the trenches all those years with me, who remembers the years of infertility and the elation that came later as we heard those monitors whir with strong healthy heartbeats. He's not here to rejoice with me when the doctor gave the all clear. Give me peace, give me comfort, let me savor in the good news and not wallow in the missing piece.

This day was so hard!

I am so thankful for **my** "heart specialist" and that I can turn to Him on days like today. He softens the blow by whispering sweet words in my ears. He reassures me. He searches out my heart. He hears me. He cares. His love draws me in and comforts me.

Today was hard even though it ended with good news. So grateful for this good news!

Scripture gives us good news as widows!

Remember no more the reproach (disappointment) of your widowhood. For your Maker is your husband--the LORD Almighty is His name—the Holy One of Israel is your Redeemer, He is called the God of all the earth.

Isaiah 54:5 NIV

Lord, thank You for being my "heart specialist" and my husband every day. Today You rejoice with me, encourage me, and comfort me when I really ached for my earthly husband. In

Your Matchless Name, Amen.

November 27
A Roadmap Out of Grief
By Kit Hinkle

> *But we do not want you to be uninformed, brothers,*
> *about those who are asleep,*
> *that you may not grieve as others do who have no hope.*
> *1 Thessalonians 4:13 ESV*

Do you ever feel like you wish someone would just hand you a roadmap and tell you how long this journey out of sorrow is supposed to take?

The world does, and as usual, the world falls short. After all, hasn't it fallen short ever since Adam and Eve bit that fruit in the Garden of Eden?

Sisters, have you ever heard of the Kubler-Ross stages of grief? As a model well-worn by psychologists around the world, it has gained acceptance as the most valid, relevant model for each of us. It basically goes like this—when a person is facing loss, they go through stages like so: denial, anger, bargaining, depression, and then acceptance.

I've always just shrugged my shoulders and gone along with this model, simply because it shows up everywhere—from grief counseling articles to mainstream media. If the world repeats it, then it must be right…. Right?

I suppose it's easy to think so, until you walk through loss yourself and somehow, these stages of grief don't quite fit.

In this ministry, I witness some widows moving past their grief, ready for the next purpose in life, while others get stuck far longer in anger or depression.

Why is that?

Is it because they loved their husband more or the loss was worse? I don't think so.

In fact, after hearing from many widows, I'm convinced that there is little connection between the level of adoration or bond between a couple and the recovery process when one of them dies.

I discovered there is something significant that Kubler-Ross was missing in her model.

Hope.

So how about entering the redeeming power of Christ into the model? Because, ladies, that's what seems to make the difference in whether grief leads to healing and a new life, or whether someone gets stuck in despair.

As I researched further, I learned that Christian counselors are beginning to take note of what's missing from the Kubler-Ross model and improve on it, for the sake of their clients.

This is so eye opening to me that all I can do is reflect back to what Paul said to the Thessalonians in our verse.

"that you may not grieve as others do who have no hope"

Sisters, are you processing your loss in the hope of Christ?

Can you see the difference between grieving in the knowledge that Christ offers everlasting life, and that this life, with all its failings and sufferings, is not our eternal home?

This life, while suffering or not, might as well be lived out with purpose. Grieving like those with no hope not only makes you miserable, but keeps you from using whatever time you have left on this planet to make an impact that will last an eternity!

My final thoughts on the founder of the Kubler-Ross model. It's one thing for an intellectual academic to spend her career studying others going through loss. But when she herself finally had to deal with her impending death, she wasn't looking forward to her eternal life. Rather, this lost soul sat in despair, unable to accept her predicament of neither having died yet nor having her old life back. How tragic and unnecessary! This isn't a criticism of her personally—more a compassionate observation of someone who suffered because the hope of Christ never reached her heart.

Has it reached yours? Sisters, I offer to you that if you have never understood how it is that Christ redeems through His act on the cross and how that changes everything for your healing process, that you make that redemption yours today.

If you have accepted this redemption, are you grieving with Hope? Embrace this Hope today and use what time you have left on this planet to make an eternal impact.

November 28

One Million Tears
By Liz Anne Wright

…a time to weep and a time to laugh,
a time to mourn and a time to dance…
Ecclesiastes 3:4 NIV

It was about a month after my husband had passed away, the boys and I were talking, and it quickly turned into reminiscing about their dad. Matthew, my then-six year old started to tell a story about his dad. My oldest son, nine at the time, shot him a look, and Matthew stopped talking.

"What's up, guys?" I asked.

"We don't want to make you cry, Mom."

"Oh, honey," I said. "Mom's gonna cry. There is no way around that. I have about a million tears I have to cry. They just have to come out. Nothing you say or don't say is going to stop that. We need to talk about Dad…and we need to cry."

As the months continued, I would periodically give them a "tear update"…how far we were into the million.

They are not all gone; I still have more tears to cry…six and a half years later. Not as often, not as hard (usually), but they are still there…and they still need to come out.

Research shows that tears have great value. Our eyes wouldn't physically work without them. They keep our eyeballs hydrated, they have an antiseptic value to protect the eye from irritants that enter, and they work to get those irritants out.

Research also shows there is another value to our tears…stress relief. Emotional tears have been shown to purge chemicals from the body that are released during stress…which helps the body get back to chemical balance.

Even Jesus cried when His good friend Lazarus died – even though He knew He would raise him again (see John 11:34-36).

One of the best pieces of advice that I received the week Keith died was from a dear widow friend. She came up to me, took my hands in hers, and said, "Cry whenever you feel like it…in the grocery, in front of the kids, wherever. You need to."

God made these tears. He knew they were coming, just as He knew Keith would be joining Him in Heaven…just as He knew that this life without Keith, while hard, would be more than enduring…it would be learning to live again.

I pray that wherever you are in your million-tear count, dear sisters, you can feel the presence of the Lord in them, and that you have the strength to carry on through them.

Dear Father, there are many, many tears in this journey of widowhood. Sometimes it is very hard to cry them all. Please give me the strength to cry when I need to, regardless of where I am and who will see. If Jesus cried tears of grief over a death, then I guess it is OK for me, also. Please help me to not bottle up my emotions, but to understand that all of them come from You. In Jesus' Name, Amen.

November 29

The Window
By Rene Zonner

Wait for the Lord;
be strong and take heart
and wait for the Lord

Psalm 27:14NIV

As the saying goes, "When God closes a door, He opens a window." But does He always?

My husband's death certainly was a closed door in my life. I had been a wife for fourteen years, I was raising three kids and moving along quite comfortably. Then the door slammed in my face. I knew that I needed to spend time, right where I was, in order to heal. And I was okay with that…for a time.

But then I started to get antsy. I was ready to move forward. I didn't want to be associated with the word "widow" any more. The grief room was beginning to feel stifling. I wanted God to open the window. But He didn't.

I thought I was "over it". I felt like I had worked through all my grief. And I had made great progress, but no window to a new life was opening up. I found myself frustrated with God. Couldn't He see that I was ready, that I was good to go? Why wasn't He opening up the window?

For the longest time, I focused on my questions and my frustrations. I did all the talking and no listening. Once I actually quieted my heart and allowed God to speak, I learned something. I learned that I wasn't as healed and ready to move on as I thought.

There were still areas in my journey that God needed me to work on. I learned that there were hurts that hadn't even surfaced yet - things that needed to be dealt with before I could move to the next thing. I was in such a hurry to move past the tragedy and be whole again that I was actually hurting my healing process.

If you are like me, it is hard to wait. Maybe, like me, you just want to move past the hurt, you want to be healed and "happy" again. But please learn from my mistake. Don't rush this process.

Grief goes so much deeper than we realize. Many times the grief over losing our spouse is just the tip of the iceberg. There may be unresolved issues, hurts that were never expressed, questions that arise after the death. Grief is complex, messy, and just can't be rushed.

The good news is this....the window does eventually open. As God revealed areas I need to work on, I strengthened and grew in my faith. I am so much better now than when I *thought* I was "over it" all. As a result, windows are opening in areas that I never would have imagined. There are some that God is keeping shut for now. I can see them, occasionally I even get a glimpse of what's on the other side. It's still hard at times but I am much better at the waiting now: waiting on God to do His thing in my life, waiting on His timing to tell me when I'm ready to move.

God will open the window, but only in His timing. Until then, "Wait for the Lord; be strong and take heart and wait for the Lord," (Psalm 27:14)

Father, I am waiting for the window to open. I ask that You

*open my heart to what You may be trying to tell me as I wait.
I pray for strength to keep still as I wait for Your perfect
timing. Encourage me and remind me that You have not
forgotten me. Thank You, Lord, for Your faithfulness to me
in my grief and healing. Amen*

November 30
Mighty Warrior Princess
By Elizabeth Dyer

*When the angel of the Lord appeared to Gideon, he said,
"The Lord is with you, mighty warrior."
"Pardon me, my lord," Gideon replied,
"but if the Lord is with us,
why has all this happened to us?
Where are all his wonders that our ancestors told us about
when they said, 'Did not the Lord bring us up out of Egypt?'
But now the Lord has abandoned us
and given us into the hand of Midian."
The Lord turned to him and said,
"Go in the strength you have
and save Israel out of Midian's hand.
Am I not sending you?"
"Pardon me, my lord," Gideon replied,
"but how can I save Israel? ... "
The Lord answered, "I will be with you..."*
Judges 6:12-16 NIV

Isn't it interesting when you find irony in
Scripture? This is one of those stories. I love that the
Angel of the Lord met Gideon where he was (hiding

from the enemy so he could thresh his grain without being attacked). It must have almost been tongue in cheek…Mighty Warrior? Who was He kidding?!!

Maybe God is saying that about you and me.

"The Lord is with you, Mighty Warrior Princess!"

And I have certainly said what Gideon said next. "Pardon me, Lord, but if you were with me, why have all these bad things happened to us? Or have you not noticed?" I certainly felt abandoned by God during certain events in my life.

My story here today isn't so much of the death of my husband, although that is huge, but what preceded that event. I went through nearly two years of struggling with my faith during the time just before my husband passed away. I felt like God had abandoned me, even as I continued attending Bible study and church and reading a devotional with my family around the table at dinner. Inside I was dying. Why had God abandoned me when I needed Him most? I was hiding in my own grain threshing floor. Hiding from all the mess that was falling out around me. Hiding in a pit that was created by someone else's decisions. Hiding from the promises of Scripture.

But God calls to me, "Greetings Warrior Princess. "

Warrior Princess? More like Worrier Princess. I look around me to see who else He is talking to!

I was dealing with my own "enemy" of doubt in God's love, dealing with unbelief and anger, and faking my happiness so no one would know of my pain. Your "enemy" might be people who once were part of your life but are now abandoning you. It could be loneliness and bitterness. Perhaps it is fear and worry. We all have "enemies" from whom we hide.

And when we are hiding away, we cannot be used effectively for the Kingdom. Gideon could not fight any of the Midians while he was hiding. He would not lead a group of warriors. He was not fit for battle.

When I was struggling with my faith, I couldn't sing those praise songs or hymns at church about how God is good and how I loved God. I was pretty mad at God, frankly. Have you dealt with anger at God for taking your husband away? I was stuck in the response that Gideon gave when he was questioning the Angel of the Lord. "Why?"

I had to come to the point where I could say, like Job, The Lord gives and the Lord takes away. Blessed be His Name. It may seem simplistic but I had to go back to what I KNEW to be true about God, regardless of my circumstances. Ladies, that is tough to do when you are angry. Feelings are so deceptive. I did not feel like God loved me. I did not feel blessed by God. I did not feel happy.

Then God said, in response to Gideon's "pardon me", to use the strength he had. I often feel like the strength I have is next to nothing. That is what makes God's next response so wonderful. "And I will be with you."

Sister , that is God's response to you and me today. And God will be with _(your name here)_____.

- What are you hiding from?

Fear.
Someone.
Worry.

Financial issues.
- What ironic label is God using on you?

Brave One.
Blessed One.
Faithful One.
Joyful One.
Loved One.
Peaceful One.
Leading One.
Teaching One.
Writing One.
Secure One.
Courageous One.
Forgiving One.
Praying One.

Maybe God has shown you a different name. Share it with us! We want to rejoice with you. Let's grasp ahold of our Ironic Names and see how God will use it to further His Kingdom. That is our purpose, anyway, right?

Father God, Thank You for giving me a new name. Guide me as I go in Your strength to fight the enemy. Remind me that this is Your battle and not my own. You will go with me. Help me not to dwell on the past and on the feelings that can't be trusted. Keep my mind focused on the Truth of Scripture. Amen

Connect With Us!

We hope you enjoyed these daily devotions. We have more ways to connect with A Widow's Might/aNew Season Ministries.

- **Social Media**: twitter(@anewseas, @AWidowsmight); facebook (aNew Season Ministries, A Widow's Might)

- **Website**: **www.anewseason.net**

- **Conference**: November, 2014 Myrtle Beach

- **Retreats**: Ruth Training Retreats

- **Blogs:** Be a **Guest Blogger** (request info on our website)

- **Prayer requests** can be submitted on our facebook page or on our website

Coming Soon: the next season of daily devotions! Look for the **Advent Edition** in the fall of 2014 aNew Season Ministries Presents...

aNew Season Widow's Conference
Novemeber 7-9, 2014
Myrtle Beach, SC

www.anewseason.net

Please join us for a weekend of discovering
and celebrating the season you are in as you
walk this grief journey. aNew Season Widows
Conference is a weekend-long event where
our writer and speaker team will share the
healing heart of Christ. We will come
together as a community of women who have
experienced loss and understand and can
minister to each other in a way that no one
else can. aNew Season Widows Conference
offers insights and approaches to the
difficult process of healing borne out of
years of applying biblical truths that place a
woman on solid ground with the Father in
Heaven Who is the Defender of widows
(Psalm 68:5).

Conference Speakers Include:

Also Available:
For the Love of <u>HER</u> Life
~ Summer Edition~

Topical/Author Index

Made in the USA
Coppell, TX
04 October 2021

63488323R00152